www.EffortlessMath.com

... So Much More Online!

✓ FREE HSPT Math lessons

✓ More HSPT Math learning books!

✓ HSPT Mathematics Worksheets

✓ Online Math Tutors

Need a PDF version of this book?

Please visit www.EffortlessMath.com

5 HSPT Math Practice Tests

Extra Practice to Help Achieve an Excellent Score

By

Reza Nazari

Published by: Effortless Math Education

www.EffortlessMath.com

Description

5 HSPT Math Practice Tests, which reflects the 2020 and 2021 test guidelines, is a comprehensive practice book to help you hone your math skills, overcome your exam anxiety, and boost your confidence -- and do your best to succeed on the HSPT Math Test. Five complete and realistic HSPT Math practice tests help you learn how the test is structured and what mathematics concepts you need to master before the test day. The practice test questions are followed by detailed answers and explanations to help you find your weak areas, learn from your mistakes, and raise your HSPT Math score.

The surest way to succeed on HSPT Math Test is with intensive practice in every math topic tested-- and that's what you will get in *5 HSPT Math Practice Tests*. This HSPT Math new edition has been updated to replicate questions appearing on the most recent HSPT Math tests. This is a precious learning tool for HSPT Math test takers who need extra practice in math to improve their HSPT Math score. After taking the HSPT Math practice tests in this book, you will have solid foundation and adequate practice that is necessary to succeed on the HSPT Math test. **This book is your ticket to ace the HSPT Math test!**

5 HSPT Math Practice Tests includes many exciting and unique features to help you improve your test scores, including:

- Content 100% aligned with the 2020 - 2021 HSPT test
- Prepared by HSPT Math instructors and test experts
- Complete coverage of all HSPT Math concepts and topics which you will be tested
- Detailed answers and explanations for every HSPT Math practice question to help you learn from your mistakes
- 5 complete practice tests (featuring new question types) with detailed answers
- And much more!

This HSPT Math practice book and other Effortless Math Education books are used by thousands of students each year to help them review core content areas, brush-up in math, discover their strengths and weaknesses, and achieve their best scores on the HSPT test.

About the Author

Reza Nazari is the author of more than 100 Math learning books including:
– **Math and Critical Thinking Challenges:** For the Middle and High School Student
– **GRE Math in 30 Days**
– **ASVAB Math Workbook 2018 - 2019**
– **Effortless Math Education Workbooks**
– **and many more Mathematics books ...**

Reza is also an experienced Math instructor and a test–prep expert who has been tutoring students since 2008. Reza is the founder of Effortless Math Education, a tutoring company that has helped many students raise their standardized test scores—and attend the colleges of their dreams. Reza provides an individualized custom learning plan and the personalized attention that makes a difference in how students view math.

You can contact Reza via email at:
reza@EffortlessMath.com

Find Reza's professional profile at:
goo.gl/zoC9rJ

Contents

HSPT Test Review

The High School Placement Test (HSPT), also known as STS-HSPT, formulated by the Scholastic Testing Service (STS) to determine acceptance in parochial high schools.

The HSPT test consists of five multiple-choice sections:

- ✓ **Verbal Skills:** 60 questions - 16 minutes
- ✓ **Quantitative Skills:** 52 questions - 30 minutes
- ✓ **Reading:** 62 questions - 25 minutes
- ✓ **Mathematics:** 64 questions - 45 minutes
- ✓ **Language:** 60 questions - 25 minutes

Keep in mind that the Quantitative Skills and the Mathematics sections are different parts. The Quantitative Skills section contains 52 questions providing number series, geometric comparisons, and number manipulation, whereas the Mathematics part measures students' math knowledge. The Math section of the test covers arithmetic, data analysis, geometry, and algebra.

Some schools allow students to use basic calculators when taking the HSPT test.

In this section, there are five complete HSPT Mathematics Tests. Take these tests to see what score you'll be able to receive on a real HSPT test.

Good luck!

Time to refine your skill with a practice examination

Take a practice HSPT Math Test to simulate the test day experience. After you've finished, score your test using the answer key.

Before You Start

- You'll need a pencil, a timer, and scratch papers to take the test.

- After you've finished the test, review the answer key to see where you went wrong.

- Use the answer sheet provided to record your answers. (You can cut it out or photocopy it)

- You will receive 1 point for every correct answer. There is no penalty for wrong answers.

Good Luck

HSPT Mathematics
Practice Test 1

2020 - 2021

Total number of questions: 64

Total time for two parts: 45 Minutes

Calculators are not allowed for this test.

3

HSPT Mathematics Practice Test Answer Sheet

Remove (or photocopy) this answer sheet and use it to complete the practice test.

HSPT Mathematics Practice Test 1 Answer Sheet

#		#		#	
1	Ⓐ Ⓑ Ⓒ Ⓓ	26	Ⓐ Ⓑ Ⓒ Ⓓ	51	Ⓐ Ⓑ Ⓒ Ⓓ
2	Ⓐ Ⓑ Ⓒ Ⓓ	27	Ⓐ Ⓑ Ⓒ Ⓓ	52	Ⓐ Ⓑ Ⓒ Ⓓ
3	Ⓐ Ⓑ Ⓒ Ⓓ	28	Ⓐ Ⓑ Ⓒ Ⓓ	53	Ⓐ Ⓑ Ⓒ Ⓓ
4	Ⓐ Ⓑ Ⓒ Ⓓ	29	Ⓐ Ⓑ Ⓒ Ⓓ	54	Ⓐ Ⓑ Ⓒ Ⓓ
5	Ⓐ Ⓑ Ⓒ Ⓓ	30	Ⓐ Ⓑ Ⓒ Ⓓ	55	Ⓐ Ⓑ Ⓒ Ⓓ
6	Ⓐ Ⓑ Ⓒ Ⓓ	31	Ⓐ Ⓑ Ⓒ Ⓓ	56	Ⓐ Ⓑ Ⓒ Ⓓ
7	Ⓐ Ⓑ Ⓒ Ⓓ	32	Ⓐ Ⓑ Ⓒ Ⓓ	57	Ⓐ Ⓑ Ⓒ Ⓓ
8	Ⓐ Ⓑ Ⓒ Ⓓ	33	Ⓐ Ⓑ Ⓒ Ⓓ	58	Ⓐ Ⓑ Ⓒ Ⓓ
9	Ⓐ Ⓑ Ⓒ Ⓓ	34	Ⓐ Ⓑ Ⓒ Ⓓ	59	Ⓐ Ⓑ Ⓒ Ⓓ
10	Ⓐ Ⓑ Ⓒ Ⓓ	35	Ⓐ Ⓑ Ⓒ Ⓓ	60	Ⓐ Ⓑ Ⓒ Ⓓ
11	Ⓐ Ⓑ Ⓒ Ⓓ	36	Ⓐ Ⓑ Ⓒ Ⓓ	61	Ⓐ Ⓑ Ⓒ Ⓓ
12	Ⓐ Ⓑ Ⓒ Ⓓ	37	Ⓐ Ⓑ Ⓒ Ⓓ	62	Ⓐ Ⓑ Ⓒ Ⓓ
13	Ⓐ Ⓑ Ⓒ Ⓓ	38	Ⓐ Ⓑ Ⓒ Ⓓ	63	Ⓐ Ⓑ Ⓒ Ⓓ
14	Ⓐ Ⓑ Ⓒ Ⓓ	39	Ⓐ Ⓑ Ⓒ Ⓓ	64	Ⓐ Ⓑ Ⓒ Ⓓ
15	Ⓐ Ⓑ Ⓒ Ⓓ	40	Ⓐ Ⓑ Ⓒ Ⓓ		
16	Ⓐ Ⓑ Ⓒ Ⓓ	41	Ⓐ Ⓑ Ⓒ Ⓓ		
17	Ⓐ Ⓑ Ⓒ Ⓓ	42	Ⓐ Ⓑ Ⓒ Ⓓ		
18	Ⓐ Ⓑ Ⓒ Ⓓ	43	Ⓐ Ⓑ Ⓒ Ⓓ		
19	Ⓐ Ⓑ Ⓒ Ⓓ	44	Ⓐ Ⓑ Ⓒ Ⓓ		
20	Ⓐ Ⓑ Ⓒ Ⓓ	45	Ⓐ Ⓑ Ⓒ Ⓓ		
21	Ⓐ Ⓑ Ⓒ Ⓓ	46	Ⓐ Ⓑ Ⓒ Ⓓ		
22	Ⓐ Ⓑ Ⓒ Ⓓ	47	Ⓐ Ⓑ Ⓒ Ⓓ		
23	Ⓐ Ⓑ Ⓒ Ⓓ	48	Ⓐ Ⓑ Ⓒ Ⓓ		
24	Ⓐ Ⓑ Ⓒ Ⓓ	49	Ⓐ Ⓑ Ⓒ Ⓓ		
25	Ⓐ Ⓑ Ⓒ Ⓓ	50	Ⓐ Ⓑ Ⓒ Ⓓ		

1) $(x^5) \cdot (x^4) =$ ___

   A. x^{20} C. x^9

   B. x D. $2x^{12}$

2) $0.79 + 7.65 + 6.24 = ?$

   A. 13.84 C. 14.48

   B. 13.55 D. 14.68

3) Which of the following is a prime number?

   A. 7 C. 21

   B. 14 D. 35

4) The sum of two numbers is M. If one of the numbers is 14, then two times the other number would be what?

   A. $2M$ C. $2(M + 14)$

   B. $2(M - 14)$ D. $(M - 14)$

5) A circle has a diameter of 5.4 inches. What is its approximate circumference?

   A. 12.55 inches   C. 14 inches

   B. 13.20 inches   D. 17 inches

6) If $x = \frac{4}{3}$ then $\frac{1}{x} = ?$

   A. $\frac{4}{3}$ C. $\frac{3}{4}$

   B. $\frac{1}{3}$ D. $\frac{1}{2}$

7) Ella (E) is 4 years older than her friend Ava (A) who is 3 years younger than her sister Sofia (S). If E, A and S denote their ages, which one of the following represents the given information?

   A. $\begin{cases} E = A + 4 \\ S = A - 3 \end{cases}$ C. $\begin{cases} A = E + 4 \\ S = A - 3 \end{cases}$

   B. $\begin{cases} E = A + 4 \\ A = S + 3 \end{cases}$ D. $\begin{cases} E = A + 4 \\ A = S - 3 \end{cases}$

8) $18a + 20 = 38, a = ?$

    A. 1   C. 11

    B. 6   D. 12

9) If $x = 4$, then $\dfrac{2^4}{x} =$

    A. 4   C. 2

    B. 1   D. 8

10) A trash container, when empty, weighs 45 pounds. If this container is filled with a load of trash that weighs 250 pounds, what is the total weight of the container and its contents?

    A. 224 pounds   C. 295 pounds

    B. 275 pounds   D. 325 pounds

11) Solve for x: $10x - 5 = 35$

    A. 4   C. 10

    B. 35   D. 3

12) Which of the following is not a multiple of 3?

    A. 23   C. 12

    B. 24   D. 27

13) If a rectangle is 35 feet by 45 feet, what is its area?

    A. 1,575   C. 1,000

    B. 870   D. 1,250

14) What is the prime factorization of 400?

    A. $2 \times 2 \times 5 \times 5$ C. 2×5

    B. $2 \times 2 \times 2 \times \times 5 \times 5$ D. $2 \times 2 \times 2 \times 5 \times 5$

15) A writer finishes 180 pages of his manuscript in 15 hours. How many pages is his average?

    A. 12   C. 3

    B. 5   D. 9

16) $(11 + 7) \div (3^3 \div 3) =$ ___

   A. 18

   B. $\dfrac{5}{7}$

   C. 2

   D. 6

17) What's the next number in the series $\{21, 18, 15, 12, ?\}$

   A. 9

   B. 12

   C. 6

   D. 15

18) Evaluate $2x + 12$, when $x = -3$

   A. 14

   B. 12

   C. 6

   D.16

19) If $8 < x \leq 10$, then x cannot be equal to:

   A. 8

   B. 9

   C. 9.5

   D. 10

20) If $x + y = 14$, what is the value of $8x + 8y$?

   A. 112

   B. 48

   C. 104

   D. 96

21) If $5 + x \geq 18$, what is the value of $x \geq$?

   A. 3

   B. 5

   C. 13

   D. 18

22) If x is 25% percent of 350, what is x?

   A. 35

   B. 95.5

   C. 87.5

   D. 250

23) Find the average of the following numbers: $18, 14, 5, 24, 24$

   A. 16.5

   B. 17

   C. 16

   D. 10

24) Some terms in a sequence are shown below. What is the fourth term in the sequence?

$$\{2, 4, 8, \ldots, 22\}$$

    A. 14   C. 22

    B. 16   D. 34

25) Convert 0.14 to a percent.
    A. 0.014%   C. 14%

    B. 0.14%   D. 1.4%

26) In the simplest form, $\frac{14}{28}$ is:

    A. $\frac{3}{7}$ C. $\frac{1}{2}$

    B. $\frac{7}{3}$ D. $\frac{1}{14}$

27) $\frac{14}{25}$ is equal to:

    A. 5.6   C. 0.06

    B. 0.56   D. 0.6

28) What number belong in the box? $8 + \square = 5$
    A. 5   C. -3

    B. 3   D. 11

29) $\sqrt{36}$ is equal to:
    A. 6   C. 9

    B. 7   D. 14

30) Which of the following is the equivalent of 3^5?
    A. $3 \times 3 \times 3 \times 3$ C. 27

    B. $4 \times 4 \times 4$ D. 243

31) Which of the following fractions is the largest?

    A. $\frac{3}{4}$ C. $\frac{8}{9}$

    B. $\frac{2}{5}$ D. $\frac{2}{3}$

32) I've got 36 quarts of milk and my family drinks 2 gallons of milk per week. How many weeks will that last us?

    A. 2 weeks

    B. 2.5 weeks

    C. 3.25 weeks

    D. 4.5 weeks

33) If $-7a = 49$, then $a =$ _____

    A. -7

    B. 7

    C. 15

    D. 0

34) Factor this expression: $x^2 + 5x - 6$

    A. $x^2(5 + 6)$

    B. $x(x + 5 - 6)$

    C. $(x + 6)(x - 1)$

    D. $(x + 6)(x - 6)$

35) $136 \times 45 = ?$

    A. 6,120

    B. 6,670

    C. 6,167

    D. 6,607

36) If $A = 6$, $B = 4$ and $C = 5$, then $2ABC = ?$

    A. 120

    B. 18

    C. 240

    D. 360

37) A baker uses 8 eggs to bake a cake. How many cakes will he be able to bake with 152 eggs?

    A. 19

    B. 21

    C. 23

    D. 25

38) What's the area of the non-shaded part of the following figure?

    A. 192

    B. 152

    C. 40

    D. 42

39) What is the difference between 160 and 73?

    A. 233

    B. 87

    C. 12,616

    D. 1.8

40) Which of the following represents the reduced form for 2.4?

A. 4

B. $2\frac{1}{2}$

C. $\frac{24}{10}$

D. $\frac{24}{100}$

41) What is 9,823.2869 rounded to the nearest tenth?

A. 9,823.3

B. 9,823.287

C. 9,823

D. 9,823.28

42) What is the radicand in $\sqrt[3]{216}$?

A. 3

B. 72

C. 36

D. 6

43) If $x = 6$ what's the value of $6x^2 + 5x - 13$?

A. 197

B. 316

C. 416

D. 233

44) Line l passes through the point $(-1, 2)$. Which of the following CANNOT be the equation of line l?

A. $y = 1 - x$

B. $y = x + 1$

C. $x = -1$

D. $y = x + 3$

45) The circumference of a circle is 35 cm. What is the approximate radius of the circle?

A. 2.4 cm

B. 5.6 cm

C. 8.0 cm

D. 9.5 cm

46) What is the sum of $\frac{8}{12} + \frac{4}{3} + \frac{2}{6}$?

A. 2.1

B. 3

C. $2\frac{1}{3}$

D. 1

47) The number 0.8 can also represented by which of the following?

A. $\frac{8}{10}$

B. $\frac{8}{100}$

C. $\frac{8}{1,000}$

D. $\frac{8}{10,000}$

48) Which of the following is the correct calculation for 5!?

   A. 4×3 C. $1 \times 2 \times 3 \times 4$

   B. $1 \times 2 \times 3 \times 4$ D. $5 \times 4 \times 3 \times 2 \times 1$

49) If $360 \, kg$ of vegetable is packed in 90 boxes, how much vegetable will each box contain?

   A. 4   C. 7

   B. 6   D. 9

50) Julie gives 8 pieces of candy to each of her friends. If Julie gives all her candy away, which amount of candy could have been the amount she distributed?

   A. 187   C. 243

   B. 223   D. 232

51) How much greater is the value of $9x + 12$ than the value of $9x - 3$?

   A. 3   C. 15

   B. 12   D. 18

52) A woman weighs 140 pounds. She gains 20 pounds one month and 8 pounds the next month. What is her new weight?

   A. 152 pounds   C. 168 pounds

   B. 146 pounds   D. 138 pounds

53) $(x + 4)(x + 3) = ?$

   A. $x^2 - 7x + 12$ C. $x^2 + 6x + 5$

   B. $x^2 + 7x + 12$ D. $x^2 + 6x - 5$

54) What is the perimeter of the triangle in the provided diagram?

   A. 25

   B. 42,875

   C. 75

   D. 105

55) The equation of a line is given as : $y = 5x - 3$. Which of the following points does not lie on the line?

    A. $(1, 2)$ C. $(3, 18)$

    B. $(-2, -13)$ D. $(2, 7)$

56) How long is the line segment shown on the number line below?

    A. -8 C. -9

    B. 8 D. 9

-10 -9 -8 -7 -6 -5 -4 -3 -2 -1 0 1 2 3 4 5 6 7 8 9 10

57) $x^2 - 64 = 0$, x could equal:

    A. 6 C. 9

    B. 8 D. 12

58) $(x^8)^3 = ?$

    A. $2x^8$ C. x^{24}

    B. x^{22} D. x^{11}

59) In the diagram provided, what is the value of a?

    A. $180°$

    B. $160°$

    C. $145°$

    D. $45°$

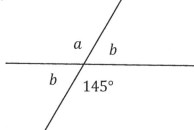

60) If a rectangular swimming pool has a perimeter of 112 feet and is 22 feet wide, what is its area?

    A. $2,496$ C. $1,464$

    B. $1,900$ D. 748

61) What is $\sqrt{25} \times \sqrt{36}$?

    A. $4\sqrt{5}$ C. 30

    B. 54 D. $\sqrt{54}$

62) The cube of 7 is ___ .

    A. 343   C. 80

    B. 64   D. 24

63) In the following figure, point Q lies on line n, what is the value of y if $x = 35$?

    A. 25

    B. 28

    C. 34

    D. 38

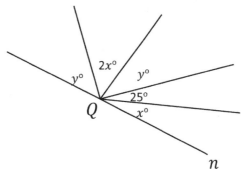

64) What's the greatest common factor of the 25 and 15?

    A. 44   C. 5

    B. 15   D. 3

STOP: This is the End of Test 1.

HSPT Mathematics
Practice Test 2

2020 - 2021

Total number of questions: 64

Total time for two parts: 45 Minutes

Calculators are not allowed for this test.

15

HSPT Mathematics Practice Test Answer Sheet

Remove (or photocopy) this answer sheet and use it to complete the practice test.

	HSPT Mathematics Practice Test 2 Answer Sheet		

1 Ⓐ Ⓑ Ⓒ Ⓓ	26 Ⓐ Ⓑ Ⓒ Ⓓ	51 Ⓐ Ⓑ Ⓒ Ⓓ	
2 Ⓐ Ⓑ Ⓒ Ⓓ	27 Ⓐ Ⓑ Ⓒ Ⓓ	52 Ⓐ Ⓑ Ⓒ Ⓓ	
3 Ⓐ Ⓑ Ⓒ Ⓓ	28 Ⓐ Ⓑ Ⓒ Ⓓ	53 Ⓐ Ⓑ Ⓒ Ⓓ	
4 Ⓐ Ⓑ Ⓒ Ⓓ	29 Ⓐ Ⓑ Ⓒ Ⓓ	54 Ⓐ Ⓑ Ⓒ Ⓓ	
5 Ⓐ Ⓑ Ⓒ Ⓓ	30 Ⓐ Ⓑ Ⓒ Ⓓ	55 Ⓐ Ⓑ Ⓒ Ⓓ	
6 Ⓐ Ⓑ Ⓒ Ⓓ	31 Ⓐ Ⓑ Ⓒ Ⓓ	56 Ⓐ Ⓑ Ⓒ Ⓓ	
7 Ⓐ Ⓑ Ⓒ Ⓓ	32 Ⓐ Ⓑ Ⓒ Ⓓ	57 Ⓐ Ⓑ Ⓒ Ⓓ	
8 Ⓐ Ⓑ Ⓒ Ⓓ	33 Ⓐ Ⓑ Ⓒ Ⓓ	58 Ⓐ Ⓑ Ⓒ Ⓓ	
9 Ⓐ Ⓑ Ⓒ Ⓓ	34 Ⓐ Ⓑ Ⓒ Ⓓ	59 Ⓐ Ⓑ Ⓒ Ⓓ	
10 Ⓐ Ⓑ Ⓒ Ⓓ	35 Ⓐ Ⓑ Ⓒ Ⓓ	60 Ⓐ Ⓑ Ⓒ Ⓓ	
11 Ⓐ Ⓑ Ⓒ Ⓓ	36 Ⓐ Ⓑ Ⓒ Ⓓ	61 Ⓐ Ⓑ Ⓒ Ⓓ	
12 Ⓐ Ⓑ Ⓒ Ⓓ	37 Ⓐ Ⓑ Ⓒ Ⓓ	62 Ⓐ Ⓑ Ⓒ Ⓓ	
13 Ⓐ Ⓑ Ⓒ Ⓓ	38 Ⓐ Ⓑ Ⓒ Ⓓ	63 Ⓐ Ⓑ Ⓒ Ⓓ	
14 Ⓐ Ⓑ Ⓒ Ⓓ	39 Ⓐ Ⓑ Ⓒ Ⓓ	64 Ⓐ Ⓑ Ⓒ Ⓓ	
15 Ⓐ Ⓑ Ⓒ Ⓓ	40 Ⓐ Ⓑ Ⓒ Ⓓ		
16 Ⓐ Ⓑ Ⓒ Ⓓ	41 Ⓐ Ⓑ Ⓒ Ⓓ		
17 Ⓐ Ⓑ Ⓒ Ⓓ	42 Ⓐ Ⓑ Ⓒ Ⓓ		
18 Ⓐ Ⓑ Ⓒ Ⓓ	43 Ⓐ Ⓑ Ⓒ Ⓓ		
19 Ⓐ Ⓑ Ⓒ Ⓓ	44 Ⓐ Ⓑ Ⓒ Ⓓ		
20 Ⓐ Ⓑ Ⓒ Ⓓ	45 Ⓐ Ⓑ Ⓒ Ⓓ		
21 Ⓐ Ⓑ Ⓒ Ⓓ	46 Ⓐ Ⓑ Ⓒ Ⓓ		
22 Ⓐ Ⓑ Ⓒ Ⓓ	47 Ⓐ Ⓑ Ⓒ Ⓓ		
23 Ⓐ Ⓑ Ⓒ Ⓓ	48 Ⓐ Ⓑ Ⓒ Ⓓ		
24 Ⓐ Ⓑ Ⓒ Ⓓ	49 Ⓐ Ⓑ Ⓒ Ⓓ		
25 Ⓐ Ⓑ Ⓒ Ⓓ	50 Ⓐ Ⓑ Ⓒ Ⓓ		

1) If $x = 6$, then $\dfrac{6^6}{x} =$

   A. 30   C. 1,296

   B. 7,776   D. 96

2) Solve for a: $8a - 15 = 9$

   A. 49   C. 32

   B. 0.45   D. 3

3) Sales price of a laptop is $1,912.50, which is 15% off the original price. What is the original price?

   A. $1,952   C. $2,250

   B. $2,000.50   D. $2,460.50

4) $\dfrac{(11\ feet\ +7\ yards)}{4} =$ ____

   A. 9 feet   C. 32 feet

   B. 8 feet   D. 4 feet

5) There are only red and blue cards in a box. The probability of choosing a red card in the box at random is one third. If there are 246 blue cards, how many cards are in the box?

   A. 123   C. 328

   B. 308   D. 369

6) Simplify the expression: $(6x^3 - 8x^2 + 2x^4) - (4x^2 - 2x^4 + 2x^3)$

   A. $4x^4 + 4x^3 - 12x^2$ C. $4x^4 + 4x^3 - 12x^2$

   B. $4x^3 - 12x^2$ D. $8x^3 - 12x^2$

7) If Emma can read a page in S minutes, what piece of the page can she read in 20 minutes?

   A. $20S$ C. $20 + S$

   B. $\dfrac{20}{S}$ D. $20 + 2S$

8) If Sam can arrange a storeroom in 2 hours, and Jim can arrange the storeroom in 3 hours, how long will it take for both of them to arrange the storeroom together?

   A. 48 minutes   C. 1 hour and 24 minutes

   B. 1 hour and 12 minutes   D. 1 hour and 36 minutes

9) Jack worked 180 hours this month and made $540. If he works 160 hours next month at the same pay rate, how much will he make?

   A. $480   C. $285

   B. $370   D. $180

10) Which of the following is an irrational number?

   A. $\sqrt{16}$ C. 0.063

   B. $\sqrt{5}$ D. -7

11) What simple interest rate will Ryan need to make $3,000 in interest on a $8,500 principal over 6 years?

   A. 3%   C. 5%

   B. 4%   D. 6%

12) 8 feet, 10 inches + 5 feet, 12 inches = how many inches?

   A. 178 inches   C. 182 inches

   B. 188 inches   D. 200 inches

13) What is the absolute value of -3?

   A. -3 C. 3

   B. 0   D. 5

14) If $(5.2 + 4.3 + 4.5)x = x$, then what is the value of x?

   A. 0   C. 1

   B. $\dfrac{1}{14}$ D. 14

15) While at work, Emma checks her email once every 60 minutes. In 9-hour, how many times does she check her email?

   A. 4 times   C. 9 times

   B. 5 times   D. 6 times

16) Which of the following is a whole number followed by its square?

   A. 2, 8   C. 4, 20

   B. 3, 9   D. 5, 30

17) $8.82 \div 2.4 = \cdots ?$

    A. 3.675   C. 3.85

    B. 3.75   D. 38.52

18) Add $22.07 + 0.035 + 14.3954 + 0.0005 + 20$?

    A. 56.42   C. 56.5009

    B. 56.4830   D. 56.6203

19) $(12 \div 4) \times (17 - 6)$?

    A. 27   C. 31

    B. 29   D. 33

20) In the circle seen below, the two lines in the circle are perpendicular. What is the value of x?

    A. 6

    B. 10

    C. 12

    D. 14

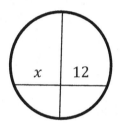

21) The sum of 8 numbers is greater than 160 and less than 240. Which of the following could be the average (arithmetic mean) of the numbers?

    A. 20   C. 30

    B. 25   D. 35

22) 58% equals:

    A. 580   C. 5.8

    B. 58   D. 0.58

23) $-20 + 6 \times (-5) - [4 + 22 \times (-4)] \div 2 = ?$

    A. -8 C. -1

    B. $\dfrac{3}{4}$ D. 8

24) There are 10 more peaches than mangoes in a basket of 48 peaches and mangoes. How many mangoes are in the basket?

    A. 31   C. 18

    B. 29   D. 15

25) Evaluate $4z + 16$, when $z = -4$

    A. -150 C. 50

    B. 16   D. 0

26) $12a + 10 = 160, a = ?$

    A. 12.5   C. 14

    B. 10   D. 18.5

27) During a fund-raiser, each of the 35 members of a group sold candy bars. If each member sold an average of five candy bars, how many total bars did the group sell?

    A. 35   C. 175

    B. 56   D. 225

28) Which of the following is a multiple of 4?

    A. 38   C. 85

    B. 46   D. 108

29) 10^5 is NOT equal to which of the following?

    A. 0.1×10^6 C. $10 \times 10 \times 10 \times 10 \times 10$

    B. 10,000   D. $10^2 \times 10^3$

30) What is the improper fraction or mixed number represented by the following figure?

    A. $\frac{5}{2}$

    B. $\frac{7}{6}$

    C. $2\frac{1}{4}$

    D. $2\frac{3}{4}$

31) What's the least common multiple (*LCM*) of 12 and 18?

A. 12 and 18 have no common multiples

B. 118

C. 112

D. 36

32) How many $\frac{1}{6}$ pound paperback books together weigh 30 pounds?

A. 85

B. 95

C. 105

D. 180

33) A woman owns a dog walking business. If 3 workers can walk 6 dogs, how many dogs can 5 workers walk?

A. 10

B. 18

C. 15

D. 25

34) Solve: $0.34 + 0.46$?

A. $\frac{3}{5}$

B. $\frac{4}{5}$

C. $\frac{2}{3}$

D. $\frac{1}{3}$

35) Emily and Daniel have taken the same number of photos on their school trip. Emily has taken 5 times as many as photos as Claire and Daniel has taken 20 more photos than Claire. How many photos has Claire taken?

A. 5

B. 6

C. 8

D. 10

36) The distance between cities A and B is approximately 2,500 miles. If you drive an average of 69 miles per hour, how many hours will it take you to drive from city A to city B?

A. approximately 41 hours

B. approximately 36 hours

C. approximately 28 hours

D. approximately 25 hours

37) If 8 garbage trucks can collect the trash of 40 homes in a day. How many trucks are needed to collect in 150 houses?

A. 15

B. 30

C. 40

D. 45

38) If $x = \frac{4}{7}$ then $\frac{1}{x} = ?$

A. $\frac{7}{4}$

B. $\frac{4}{7}$

C. 4

D. 7

39) Find the square of $\frac{4}{9}$?

A. $\frac{16}{81}$

B. $\frac{81}{16}$

C. $\frac{16}{18}$

D. $\frac{8}{81}$

40) Which of the following is NOT a factor of 50?

A. 5

B. 2

C. 10

D. 15

41) What is the place value of 2 in 4.8325?

A. hundredths

B. thousandths

C. ten thousandths

D. hundred thousandths

42) Which symbol belongs in the circle? 0.542 ◯ 0.0540

A. <

B. >

C. =

D. ≤

43) $(-25) + (-12) =.$

A. 13

B. 10

C. −26

D. −37

44) Use the diagram provided as a reference. If the length between point A and C is 68, and the length between point A and B is 25, what is the length between point B and C?

A. 41

B. 68

C. 31

D. 43

A B C

45) 0.000561 equals:

   A. 5.61×10^4 C. 5.61×10^{-3}

   B. 5.61×10^3 D. 5.61×10^{-4}

46) As a fraction, 0.36 is?

   A. $\frac{3}{36}$ C. $\frac{3}{20}$

   B. $\frac{8}{25}$ D. $\frac{9}{25}$

47) Which of the following is the correct graph for $x \geq 2$ or $x \leq -1$?

   A.

   B.

   C.

   D.

48) Jacob is having a birthday party for his girl and is serving orange juice to the 9 children in attendance. If Jacob has 1 liter of orange juice and wants to divide it equally among the children, how many liters does each child get?

   A. $\frac{1}{8}$ C. $\frac{1}{9}$

   B. $\frac{1}{7}$ D. $\frac{1}{16}$

49) If Frank needs $2\frac{1}{4}$ cup of milk to make a cake. How many cup of milk will he need to make 4 cakes?

   A. 3   C. 9

   B. 6   D. 12

50) If Ella needed to buy 4 bottles of soda for a party in which 10 people attended, how many bottles of soda will she need to buy for a party in which 5 people are attending?

    A. 2

    B. 6

    C. 10

    D. 12

51) Which of the following represents the reduced fraction form for 1.9?

    A. $2\frac{9}{10}$

    B. $1\frac{4}{5}$

    C. $\frac{19}{10}$

    D. $\frac{36}{20}$

52) If a discount of 20% off the retail price of a chair saves Anna $30. How much did she pay for the chair?

    A. $100

    B. $115

    C. $120

    D. $135

53) The fraction $\frac{5}{4}$ can also be written as which of the following?

    A. $\frac{4}{3}$

    B. 0.25

    C. 1.25

    D. 34.75

54) Which of the following is equivalent to $7 \times 7 \times 7 \times 7 \times 7$?

    A. $\sqrt{7} \times 7$

    B. 7^5

    C. $7 \div 7$

    D. 7,000

55) Emily lives $5\frac{1}{4}$ miles from where she works. When traveling to work, she walks to a bus stop $\frac{1}{3}$ of the way to catch a bus. How many miles away from her house is the bus stop?

    A. $4\frac{1}{3}$ miles

    B. $4\frac{3}{4}$ miles

    C. $2\frac{3}{4}$ miles

    D. $1\frac{3}{4}$ miles

56) A bread recipe calls for $2\frac{2}{3}$ cups of flour. If you only have $1\frac{5}{6}$ cups, how much more flour is needed?

    A. 1

    B. $\frac{1}{2}$

    C. 2

    D. $\frac{5}{6}$

57) If $l = 3$, $a = 5$ and $b = 3$, then $\frac{4lab}{5} = ?$

   A. 96   C. 48

   B. 24   D. 36

58) Mario loaned Jett $1,300 at a yearly interest rate of 5%. After two year what is the interest owned on this loan?

   A. $130   C. $5

   B. $60   D. $1260

59) In the diagram below, circle A represents the set of all odd numbers, circle B represents the set of all negative numbers, and circle C represents the set of all multiples of 5. Which number could be replaced with y?

   A. 5

   B. 0

   C. -5

   D. -10

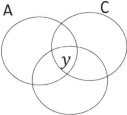

60) Charlotte is 48 years old, twice as old as Avery. How old is Avery?

   A. 24 years old   C. 20 years old

   B. 28 years old   D. 15 years old

61) In the given diagram, the height is $8\ cm$. what is the area of the triangle?

   A. $28\ cm^2$

   B. $46\ cm^2$

   C. $112\ cm^2$

   D. $252\ cm^2$

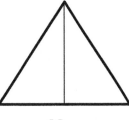

28 cm

62) In the figure below, line A is parallel to line B. What is the value of angle x?

   A. 35 degree

   B. 55 degree

   C. 100 degree

   D. 125 degree

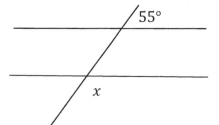

63) Mr. Carlos family are choosing a menu for their reception. They have 3 choices of appetizers, 5 choices of entrees, 4 choices of cake. How many different menu combinations are possible for them to choose

      A. 12   C. 60

      B. 32   D. 120

64) There are two pizza ovens in a restaurant. Oven 1 burns four times as many pizzas as oven 2. If the restaurant had a total of 15 burnt pizzas on Saturday, how many pizzas did oven 2 burn?

      A. 3   C. 9

      B. 6   D. 12

STOP: This is the End of Test 2.

HSPT Mathematics
Practice Test 3

2020 - 2021

Total number of questions: 64

Total time for two parts: 45 Minutes

Calculators are not allowed for this test.

27

HSPT Mathematics Practice Test Answer Sheet

Remove (or photocopy) this answer sheet and use it to complete the practice test.

	HSPT Mathematics Practice Test 3 Answer Sheet		
1 (A) (B) (C) (D)	26 (A) (B) (C) (D)	51 (A) (B) (C) (D)
2 (A) (B) (C) (D)	27 (A) (B) (C) (D)	52 (A) (B) (C) (D)
3 (A) (B) (C) (D)	28 (A) (B) (C) (D)	53 (A) (B) (C) (D)
4 (A) (B) (C) (D)	29 (A) (B) (C) (D)	54 (A) (B) (C) (D)
5 (A) (B) (C) (D)	30 (A) (B) (C) (D)	55 (A) (B) (C) (D)
6 (A) (B) (C) (D)	31 (A) (B) (C) (D)	56 (A) (B) (C) (D)
7 (A) (B) (C) (D)	32 (A) (B) (C) (D)	57 (A) (B) (C) (D)
8 (A) (B) (C) (D)	33 (A) (B) (C) (D)	58 (A) (B) (C) (D)
9 (A) (B) (C) (D)	34 (A) (B) (C) (D)	59 (A) (B) (C) (D)
10 (A) (B) (C) (D)	35 (A) (B) (C) (D)	60 (A) (B) (C) (D)
11 (A) (B) (C) (D)	36 (A) (B) (C) (D)	61 (A) (B) (C) (D)
12 (A) (B) (C) (D)	37 (A) (B) (C) (D)	62 (A) (B) (C) (D)
13 (A) (B) (C) (D)	38 (A) (B) (C) (D)	63 (A) (B) (C) (D)
14 (A) (B) (C) (D)	39 (A) (B) (C) (D)	64 (A) (B) (C) (D)
15 (A) (B) (C) (D)	40 (A) (B) (C) (D)	
16 (A) (B) (C) (D)	41 (A) (B) (C) (D)	
17 (A) (B) (C) (D)	42 (A) (B) (C) (D)	
18 (A) (B) (C) (D)	43 (A) (B) (C) (D)	
19 (A) (B) (C) (D)	44 (A) (B) (C) (D)	
20 (A) (B) (C) (D)	45 (A) (B) (C) (D)	
21 (A) (B) (C) (D)	46 (A) (B) (C) (D)	
22 (A) (B) (C) (D)	47 (A) (B) (C) (D)	
23 (A) (B) (C) (D)	48 (A) (B) (C) (D)	
24 (A) (B) (C) (D)	49 (A) (B) (C) (D)	
25 (A) (B) (C) (D)	50 (A) (B) (C) (D)	

1) Raymond wants to invest \$5,000 at 4% simple interest rate for 6 years. How much interest will he receive?

   A. \$1,200

   B. \$1,350

   C. \$1,500

   D. \$1,700

2) If $x = 4$, then $\dfrac{2^3}{x-2} =$

   A. 4

   B. 1

   C. 2

   D. 8

3) Over the course of a week, Matt spent \$35 on foods. What was the average cost per day?

   A. \$3.65

   B. \$4

   C. \$4.50

   D. \$5

4) Find $0.00832 \div 2$

   A. 0.041

   B. 0.00416

   C. 0.0416

   D. 41.6

5) $-45 + 6 - 12$ equals:

   A. 51

   B. -51

   C. -53

   D. 53

6) Multiply 10^6 by 10^3

   A. 10^7

   B. 10^8

   C. 10^9

   D. 10^{-9}

7) Find 3.48×10^5

   A. 348

   B. 3,480

   C. 34,800

   D. 348,000

8) If a circle has the diameter of 6, what is the area of the circle?

   A. 3π

   B. 6π

   C. 9π

   D. 12π

9) What percent of 120 is 45?

    A. 30%   C. 37.5%

    B. 34.5%   D. 40%

10) Find the fraction of the grid that is shaded.

    A. $\frac{2}{5}$

    B. $\frac{1}{3}$

    C. $\frac{2}{3}$

    D. $\frac{1}{2}$

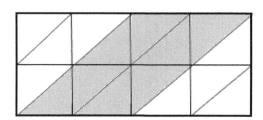

11) If a vehicle is driven 42 miles on Monday, 38 miles on Tuesday, and 34 miles on Wednesday, what is the average number of miles driven each day?

    A. 38 miles   C. 34 miles

    B. 36 miles   D. 30 miles

12) In the following right triangle, if the sides AB and AC become twice longer, what will be the ratio of the perimeter of the triangle to its area?

    A. $\frac{1}{2}$

    B. 2

    C. $\frac{1}{3}$

    D. 3

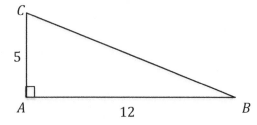

13) Which number sentence is true?

    A. $-10 + 8 > 0$ C. $|-36 - 2| = -38$

    B. $|-6 + 7| = 1$ D. $12 + 19 < -2$

14) A student gets an 85% on a test with 40 questions. How many answers did the student solve correctly?

    A. 25   C. 34

    B. 28   D. 36

15) 240 Students are in a school. $\frac{3}{5}$ Of these students are boys. How many girls are in the school?

    A. 86   C. 96

    B. 92   D. 108

16) What number is 8 less than $\frac{1}{5}$ of 45?

    A. 0   C. 3

    B. 1   D. 5

17) On a map, 1 cm represents 90 miles. How many miles apart are two cities that are $2\frac{1}{3}$ cm apart on the map?

    A. 150   C. 210

    B. 190   D. 260

18) What is the value of x?

    A. 102

    B. 108

    C. 112

    D. 120

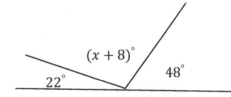

19) What number is $\frac{1}{3}$ of the mean of 5, 3, 14, 22, 12, 6, 1.

    A. 18   C. 5

    B. 10   D. 3

20) $\frac{2}{5}$ of what number is 4 times 3:

    A. 30   C. 18

    B. 26   D. 15

21) $\{2, 5, 7, 16\} \cap \{4, 5, 2, 9\} = ?$

    A. $\{2, 9\}$ C. $\{\ \ \}$

    B. $\{2\}$ D. $\{2, 5\}$

22) What number belongs in the box? $48 + \square = 43$

    A. 5   C. -5

    B. 3   D. 11

23) Simplify: : $1 + 4(-3)^4 =$

    A. -95 C. 325

    B. 186   D. 400

24) Which of the following is a pair of reciprocals?

    A. $(2\frac{1}{5}, \frac{5}{11})$ C. $(1, -1)$

    B. $(5^2, 2^5)$ D. $(-2, 2)$

25) The square root of 180 is between

    A. $13, 14$ C. $15, 16$

    B. $14, 15$ D. $16, 17$

26) $(5 + 7) \div (3^2 \div 3) =$ ___

    A. 12   C. 4

    B. $\frac{5}{7}$ D. 6

27) Solve: $3\frac{3}{8} + 9 =$

    A. $10\frac{1}{8}$ C. $12\frac{3}{7}$

    B. $12\frac{3}{8}$ D. $10\frac{3}{7}$

28) A car is on sale for $18,000, which is a 10% discount off the regular price. What is the regular price?

    A. $20,000   C. $27,000

    B. $23,000   D.$31,000

29) In the following diagram, the straight line is divided by one angled line at 108°. What is the value of a.

A. 66°

B. 90°

C. 72°

D. 180°

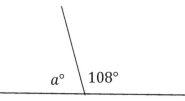

30) 15% of 40 is:

A. 9

C. 5

B. 6

D. 3

31) If $N = 2$ and $\frac{64}{N} + 4 = \square$, then $\square = \dots$.

A. 30

C. 36

B. 32

D. 46

32) Emma paid $450 for her bills last month. How much did she pay, on average, per day?

A. $9.30

C. $13.50

B. $11

D. $15

33) If $-7a = 63$, then $a = $ ___

A. -9

C. 18

B. 9

D. 0

34) If $N \times (5 - 3) = 12$ then $N = ?$

A. 6

C. 13

B. 12

D. 14

35) Which of the following is false?

A. $(x + y)z = xz + yz$

C. $(x + y) \div z = \frac{x}{z} + \frac{y}{z}$

B. $x \div y = y(\frac{1}{x})$

D. $x(y + 1) = xy + x$

36) On the number line below, point M is located on line segment ON so that $OM = \frac{1}{3}MN$. What is the position of point M?

A. 1

B. 1.5

C. 2

D. 2.5

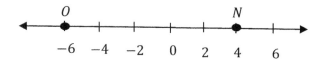

37) A circus sold 80 student tickets at $1.50 each and 200 adult tickets at $2.00 each. How much was collected?

A. $490

B. $520

C. $550

D. $630

38) Sara has $26 more than three times the amount Emma has. If Sara has $62, how much does Emma has?

A. $12

B. $18.50

C. $26.40

D. $35

39) What are the coordinates of point S on the following graph?

A. $(-2, 3)$

B. $(-3, 3)$

C. $(-3, 4)$

D. $(-1, 2)$

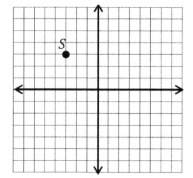

40) Which of the following is equal to 2.5?

A. 3

B. $2\frac{1}{10}$

C. $\frac{25}{10}$

D. $\frac{25}{100}$

41) If 30 is 60% of a number, what is 20% of the same number?

A. 4

B. 6

C. 8

D. 10

42) The number multiplied by 6 is 6 more than 30?

   A. 3   C. 18

   B. 6   D. 36

43) If Steve can paint a room in x hours, what part of the room he can paint in 5 hours?

   A. $\frac{x}{5}$ C. $\frac{5}{x}$

   B. $\frac{1}{5}$ D. $\frac{2}{x}$

44) Which of the following is equal to the expression below? $(2x + y)(x - 2y)$

   A. $4x^2 - 2y^2$ C. $2x^2 - 2y^2 + 2xy$

   B. $2x^2 - 2y^2$ D. $2x^2 - 2y^2 - 3xy$

45) Which answer is equivalent to five to the fifth power?

   A. 0.0005   C. 25

   B. 50,000   D. 3,125

46) The ratio of $\frac{2}{5}$ to $\frac{3}{10}$ is?

   A. 1 to 3   C. 3 to 3

   B. 2 to 3   D. 4 to 3

47) Solve for x: $\left(\frac{5}{4} + \frac{2}{3}\right) - \left(\frac{1}{2} - \frac{1}{3}\right) = x$

   A. $\frac{1}{4}$ C. $2\frac{1}{4}$

   B. $1\frac{3}{4}$ D. $2\frac{3}{4}$

48) $(x + 2)(x + 3) = ?$

   A. $x^2 - 3x + 6$ C. $x^2 + 6x + 5$

   B. $x^2 + 5x + 6$ D. $x^2 + 6x - 5$

49) Examine (X), (Y), and (Z) and find the best answer?

$(X) = 5^2$, $(Y) = 3 \times 8$, $(Z) = (5 \times 3) + 10$

   A. $(X) = (Y)$ and both are smaller than (Z)

   B. $(X) = (Z)$ and both are greater than (Y)

   C. $(X) + (Y) = (Z)$

   D. $(Y) + (Z) = (X)$

50) $(x^6)^4 = ?$

   A. $2x^6$ C. x^{24}

   B. x^2 D. x^{10}

51) $\dfrac{(8\ feet\ +8\ yards)}{4} = $ ____

   A. 9 feet   C. 32 feet

   B. 8 feet   D. 4 feet

52) Kim spent \$35 for pants. This was \$10 less than triple what she spent for a shirt. How much was the shirt?

   A. \$11   C. \$15

   B. \$13   D. \$17

53) $\dfrac{4 \times 9}{5 \times 12} = ?$

   A. $\dfrac{3}{5}$ C. $\dfrac{2}{5}$

   B. $\dfrac{3}{4}$ D. $\dfrac{1}{3}$

54) Four hundred thirty-five million eight hundred thousand seven hundred fifteen $= ?$

   A. 435,860,715   C. 435,800,715

   B. 4,247,715   D. 43,174,715

55) If $a > 6$, then

   A. $a^2 < 5$ C. $a^2 + 6 < 40$

   B. $a^2 > 34$ D. $a^2 - 6 < 28$

56) How many fourths are there in $\frac{5}{8}$?

    A. 4

    B. $2\frac{1}{2}$

    C. $3\frac{1}{8}$

    D. $2\frac{3}{2}$

57) Write 867 in expended form, using exponents.

    A. $(8 \times 10^3) + (6 \times 10^2) + 7$

    B. $(8 \times 10^2) + (6 \times 10) + 7$

    C. $(8 \times 10^3) + (6 \times 10^2) + (7 \times 10)$

    D. $(8 \times 10^3) + (6 \times 10) + 7$

58) The ratio of doctors to nurses in a hospital is $1:3$. If there are 24 doctors in the hospital, how many nurses are there?

    A. 8

    B. 24

    C. 46

    D. 72

59) If $x = 6$, $y = 3$, and $z = 5$, the value of $\sqrt{3y + 2z + x}$ is

    A. 5

    B. $\sqrt{28}$

    C. 9

    D. 15

60) 6 is to 48 as $\frac{3}{8}$ is to?

    A. 3

    B. 6

    C. $\frac{5}{8}$

    D. 8

61) What is the radicand in $\sqrt[3]{216}$?

    A. 3

    B. 72

    C. 36

    D. 6

62) If $x = 7$ what's the value of $6x^2 + 5x - 13$?

    A. 64

    B. 316

    C. 416

    D. 293

63) What is the difference between $(6 \times 10^2) + (2 \times 10)$ and $(7 \times 10^3) + 9$?

    A. 620

    B. 3,326

    C. 6,389

    D. 7,721

64) Find the area of a triangle whose dimensions are $b = 10\ cm,\ h = 16\ cm$?

A. $45\ cm^2$

C. $96\ cm^2$

B. $80\ cm^2$

D. $180\ cm^2$

STOP: This is the End of Test 3.

HSPT Mathematics Practice Test 4

2020 - 2021

Total number of questions: 64

Total time for two parts: 45 Minutes

Calculators are not allowed for this test.

39

HSPT Mathematics Practice Test Answer Sheet

Remove (or photocopy) this answer sheet and use it to complete the practice test.

	HSPT Mathematics Practice Test 4 Answer Sheet	
1 Ⓐ Ⓑ Ⓒ Ⓓ	26 Ⓐ Ⓑ Ⓒ Ⓓ	51 Ⓐ Ⓑ Ⓒ Ⓓ
2 Ⓐ Ⓑ Ⓒ Ⓓ	27 Ⓐ Ⓑ Ⓒ Ⓓ	52 Ⓐ Ⓑ Ⓒ Ⓓ
3 Ⓐ Ⓑ Ⓒ Ⓓ	28 Ⓐ Ⓑ Ⓒ Ⓓ	53 Ⓐ Ⓑ Ⓒ Ⓓ
4 Ⓐ Ⓑ Ⓒ Ⓓ	29 Ⓐ Ⓑ Ⓒ Ⓓ	54 Ⓐ Ⓑ Ⓒ Ⓓ
5 Ⓐ Ⓑ Ⓒ Ⓓ	30 Ⓐ Ⓑ Ⓒ Ⓓ	55 Ⓐ Ⓑ Ⓒ Ⓓ
6 Ⓐ Ⓑ Ⓒ Ⓓ	31 Ⓐ Ⓑ Ⓒ Ⓓ	56 Ⓐ Ⓑ Ⓒ Ⓓ
7 Ⓐ Ⓑ Ⓒ Ⓓ	32 Ⓐ Ⓑ Ⓒ Ⓓ	57 Ⓐ Ⓑ Ⓒ Ⓓ
8 Ⓐ Ⓑ Ⓒ Ⓓ	33 Ⓐ Ⓑ Ⓒ Ⓓ	58 Ⓐ Ⓑ Ⓒ Ⓓ
9 Ⓐ Ⓑ Ⓒ Ⓓ	34 Ⓐ Ⓑ Ⓒ Ⓓ	59 Ⓐ Ⓑ Ⓒ Ⓓ
10 Ⓐ Ⓑ Ⓒ Ⓓ	35 Ⓐ Ⓑ Ⓒ Ⓓ	60 Ⓐ Ⓑ Ⓒ Ⓓ
11 Ⓐ Ⓑ Ⓒ Ⓓ	36 Ⓐ Ⓑ Ⓒ Ⓓ	61 Ⓐ Ⓑ Ⓒ Ⓓ
12 Ⓐ Ⓑ Ⓒ Ⓓ	37 Ⓐ Ⓑ Ⓒ Ⓓ	62 Ⓐ Ⓑ Ⓒ Ⓓ
13 Ⓐ Ⓑ Ⓒ Ⓓ	38 Ⓐ Ⓑ Ⓒ Ⓓ	63 Ⓐ Ⓑ Ⓒ Ⓓ
14 Ⓐ Ⓑ Ⓒ Ⓓ	39 Ⓐ Ⓑ Ⓒ Ⓓ	64 Ⓐ Ⓑ Ⓒ Ⓓ
15 Ⓐ Ⓑ Ⓒ Ⓓ	40 Ⓐ Ⓑ Ⓒ Ⓓ	
16 Ⓐ Ⓑ Ⓒ Ⓓ	41 Ⓐ Ⓑ Ⓒ Ⓓ	
17 Ⓐ Ⓑ Ⓒ Ⓓ	42 Ⓐ Ⓑ Ⓒ Ⓓ	
18 Ⓐ Ⓑ Ⓒ Ⓓ	43 Ⓐ Ⓑ Ⓒ Ⓓ	
19 Ⓐ Ⓑ Ⓒ Ⓓ	44 Ⓐ Ⓑ Ⓒ Ⓓ	
20 Ⓐ Ⓑ Ⓒ Ⓓ	45 Ⓐ Ⓑ Ⓒ Ⓓ	
21 Ⓐ Ⓑ Ⓒ Ⓓ	46 Ⓐ Ⓑ Ⓒ Ⓓ	
22 Ⓐ Ⓑ Ⓒ Ⓓ	47 Ⓐ Ⓑ Ⓒ Ⓓ	
23 Ⓐ Ⓑ Ⓒ Ⓓ	48 Ⓐ Ⓑ Ⓒ Ⓓ	
24 Ⓐ Ⓑ Ⓒ Ⓓ	49 Ⓐ Ⓑ Ⓒ Ⓓ	
25 Ⓐ Ⓑ Ⓒ Ⓓ	50 Ⓐ Ⓑ Ⓒ Ⓓ	

1) Solve the following equation for x: $\frac{5x}{7} = 10 - 5x$?

   A. 1

   B. 3

   C. 5

   D. $\frac{7}{4}$

2) The following table represents the value of x and function $f(x)$. Which of the following could be the equation of the function $f(x)$?

   A. $f(x) = x^2 - 5$

   B. $f(x) = x^2 - 1$

   C. $f(x) = \sqrt{x + 2}$

   D. $f(x) = \sqrt{x} + 4$

x	$f(x)$
1	5
4	6
9	7
16	8

3) If $a = 4x$ then $8x = 2b$, then $a =$?

   A. $b - 1$

   B. b

   C. $2b$

   D. $2b + 1$

4) Divide a^4 by a^2?

   A. a^2

   B. a^4

   C. a^6

   D. a^8

5) $-18 + 6 \times (-5) - [4 + 22 \times (-4)] \div 2 = $?

   A. -6

   B. $\frac{3}{4}$

   C. -1

   D. 6

6) 250,000 equals:

   A. 2.5×10^4

   B. 2.5×10^5

   C. 25×10^4

   D. 25×10^5

7) How many years does Mary need to invest her \$4,000 at 5% to earn \$200 in simple interest?

   A. 8 yeras

   B. 5 years

   C. 3 years

   D. 1 year

8) What is the measure of angle y in the figure below if angle x measures $32°$?

A. $48°$

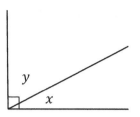

B. $54°$

C. $58°$

D. $63°$

9) Which of the following is not a factor of 45?

A. 3   C. 9

B. 5   D. 12

10) Solve: $10 - 3\frac{4}{9} = ?$

A. $6\frac{5}{9}$ C. $2\frac{5}{9}$

B. $3\frac{2}{9}$ D. $1\frac{3}{9}$

11) If the 4% sales tax on a laptop was $50, what was the price of the laptop not including the tax?

A. $1,250   C. $840

B. $986   D. $725

12) If 12 is added to an integer, and the result is $\frac{8}{7}$ of the integer, what is the integer?

A. 84   C. -56

B. 56   D. -84

13) Two years ago, Mark's father was 3 times as old as Mark. How old is Mark's father now if Mark is 20?

A. 18   C. 40

B. 36   D. 56

14) If $x = 4$, $y = 6$, and $z = 5$, then $\frac{2yz}{3x} = ?$

A. 5   C. $2\frac{2}{5}$

B. $\frac{1}{3}$ D. 15

15) What number is 5 less than the cube of 6 divided by 6?

    A. 16   C. 31

    B. 25   D. 44

16) What two numbers should come next in the following series: 24, 29, 35, 42, …?

    A. 43, 47   C. 50, 59

    B. 44, 46   D. 52, 55

17) By how much does the average of 24, 16, 65, and 88 exceed 38?

    A. 11   C. 33

    B. 28   D. 49

18) The sum of 40% of a number and 20% of the same number is 84. What is the number?

    A. 96.4   C. 137

    B. 115   D. 140

19) $2^5 \times 6^3 =$

    A. $2 \times 2 \times 2 \times 2 \times 6 \times 6 \times 5$ C. $2 \times 2 \times 2 \times 2 \times 6 \times 6 \times 18$

    B. $2 \times 2 \times 2 \times 2 \times 6 \times 6 \times 10$ D. $2 \times 2 \times 2 \times 6 \times 6 \times 6 \times 6 \times 6$

20) What is the value of x in the figure below?

    A. $44°$

    B. $46°$

    C. $48°$

    D. $50°$

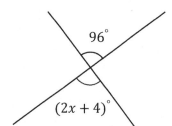

21) Which symbol belongs in the box? 0.0058 □ 0.036

    A. $<$ C. $\cong$

    B. $>$ D. $=$

22) Solve for x: $x^2 + 14 = 50$?

    A. ± 6 C. ± 32

    B. ± 24 D. ± 64

23) The angle of the shaded area in the circle is $MON = 30°$. What fraction of the circle is shaded?

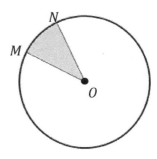

    A. $\frac{2}{5}$

    B. $\frac{1}{12}$

    C. $\frac{3}{11}$

    D. $\frac{4}{9}$

24) The area of the square shown is $144\ cm^2$. What is x?

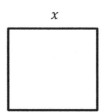

    A. $12\ cm$

    B. $10\ cm$

    C. $8\ cm$

    D. $6\ cm$

25) What is the value of the following expression? $|-5| + 9 \times 2\frac{1}{3} + (-3)^2$

    A. 30   C. 40

    B. 35   D. 45

26) Which set of angle measures can be the angle measures of triangle?

    A. $35, 45, 90$ C. $100, 35, 40$

    B. $65, 70, 80$ D. $40, 50, 90$

27) Which list shows the numbers in order from greatest value to least value?

    A. $\frac{3}{4}, \frac{2}{3}, \frac{4}{7}, \frac{1}{2}, \frac{2}{5}$ C. $, \frac{1}{2}, \frac{2}{5}, \frac{3}{4}, \frac{2}{3}, \frac{4}{7}$

    B. $\frac{4}{7}, \frac{1}{2}, \frac{2}{5}, \frac{3}{4}, \frac{2}{3}$ D. $\frac{3}{4}, \frac{2}{5}, \frac{4}{7}, \frac{2}{3}, \frac{1}{2}$

28) Which expression is equivalent to $-12 + (5 \times n)$?

    A. $12n - 5$ C. $5n$

    B. $5n - 12$ D. $n - 12$

29) Which inequality is true if $x = 2.5$?

    A. $3x > 9.5$ C. $2x < 6$

    B. $4x = 9.78$ D. $5x - 1 > 12$

30) An experimenter used $650\ ml$ of alcohol for an experiment. How many liters of the alcohol did the experimenter use for this experiment?

    A. 65 C. 0.065

    B. 0.65 D. 0.0065

31) The ratio of the number of boys to girls in a class is 3 to 2. There are 27 boys in the class. How many girl are in the class?

    A. 18 C. 25

    B. 20 D. 32

32) Three points are labeled on the number line. Which point represents the value of $\left|-\frac{3}{2}\right|$?

    A. A

    B. B

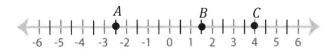

    C. C

    D. None

33) What is the range of the following numbers? $12, 3, 5, 6, 18, 25, 27, 36, 9$?

    A. 22 C. 33

    B. 27 D. 38

34) What is the value of $\frac{5}{18} \times \frac{9}{60}$?

    A. $\frac{2}{27}$ C. $\frac{1}{23}$

    B. $\frac{3}{25}$ D. $\frac{1}{24}$

35) Which expression has a value of -34?

    A. $2(5 - 1) + 5$ C. $12 + 8(13) - 5$

    B. $14 - 6(6) - 12$ D. $28 - 56 + 10$

36) The area of a triangle is 36 square inches. The base of the triangle is 4 inches. What is the height of the triangle in inches.

    A. 10 in C. 18 in

    B. 14.5 in D. 22.4 in

37) $\frac{5}{8}$ of people who attended a concert arrived late. What percentage is equivalent to the fraction of people who arrived late.

    A. 45%   C. 58.25%

    B. 52.5%   D. 62.5%

38) A tree's height is 2 meter 40 centimeters. How tall is the tree in millimeters?

    A. 1,800 mm C. 2,400 mm

    B. 2,100 mm D. 2,700 mm

39) Which two expressions are equivalent?

    A. $2(x + 3)$ and $2x + 5$ C. $(18 \div 2) + 1$ and $(18 + 2) \div 1$

    B. $2x - 5 + 8 + 5x$ and $7x + 3$ D. $2 + (6 \times 4)$ and $(6 + 4) \times 2$

40) What is the square root of 64?

    A. 6   C. 9

    B. 8   D. 4,096

41) At the weekend, Alfred drank a total of 13 fluid ounces of milk. If he drank p fluid ounces of milk on Saturday morning, which equation can be used to find q, the number of fluid ounces of milk he drank the rest of the weekend?

    A. $13 - p = q$ C. $13 \times p \div 2 = q$

    B. $13 + p = q$ D. $13 \div p = q$

42) The diameter of a circle is 18 centimeters. Which expression can be used to find the area of the circle in centimeters?

    A. $\pi \times 8$ C. $\pi \times 18$

    B. $\pi \times 9$ D. $\pi \times 81$

43) If $a = 4$ then $a^a . a =$?

    A. 40   C. 1,024

    B. 256   D. $4x$

44) Each of four students wrote an equation.

    • Stevie wrote $1\frac{5}{7} = \frac{12}{7}$

    • Marc wrote $2\frac{2}{3} = \frac{16}{9}$

    • Tom wrote $1.05 = \frac{105}{10}$

    • John wrote $\frac{7}{3} = 2\frac{1}{3}$

Which of these students wrote an equation that is false?

    A. Stevie only

    B. Marc only

    C. Tom and Marc only

    D. John, Tom and Marc

45) If $7 + 2x \leq 15$, then $x \leq$?

    A. $14x$ C. -4

    B. 4   D. $15x$

46) Kevin and Nicole both started running a race at $9:30\ A.M.$ Kevin finished the race in 2 hours 15 minutes. Nicole finished the race in 1 hour 40 minutes after Kevin did. At what time did Nicole finish the race?

    A. $3:55\ P.M$ C. $1:25\ P.M$

    B. $12:45\ P.M$ D. Not here

47) On a test, Tom had to answer 18 questions. He earned 3.5 points for every question he answered correctly. Which equation can be used to find t, the total number of points Tom earned for answering q questions correctly?

    A. $t = q(18 - 3.5)$ C. $t = 3.5(18 - q)$

    B. $t = 3.5q$ D. $t = 3.5 \times 18 + q$

48) Which model is shaded to best represent the following expression: $\frac{2}{6} + \frac{3}{4}$

A. 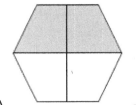 +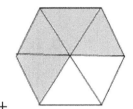

B. 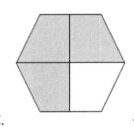 +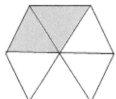

C. 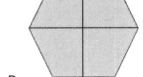 +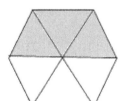

D.

49) The number of pens in different boxes are shown below.

$$14, 32, 20, 42, 45, 13, 36, 8, 28, 32$$

What is the median number pens in the boxes?

A. 24   C. 31

B. 30   D. 35

50) What is an example of a pair of consecutive numbers?

A. 6, 6   C. 7, 8

B. $\frac{5}{2}, \frac{2}{5}$ D. $-3, 3$

51) What fraction has a value between $\frac{1}{4}$ and $\frac{3}{4}$?

    A. $\frac{1}{3}$ C. $\frac{2}{5}$

    B. $\frac{1}{2}$ D. $\frac{7}{4}$

52) What proportions must be true if triangle ABC and triangle AGH are similar?

    A. $\frac{AB}{AG} = \frac{AH}{GH}$

    B. $\frac{AG}{GB} = \frac{BC}{GH}$

    C. $\frac{AB}{AG} = \frac{BC}{GH}$

    D. $\frac{AH}{AG} = \frac{BC}{GH}$

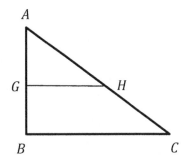

53) Brad bought 5 pens at \$2.40 each and 3 erasers at \$3.50 each. How much did he spend?

    A. \$18.36   C. \$37.50

    B. \$22.50   D. \$39.30

54) Which of these is an example of the associative property of addition?

    A. $\frac{1}{7} + \frac{2}{7} = \frac{3}{7}$ C. $\frac{5}{4} + \frac{3}{4} = 2$

    B. $\left(\frac{2}{5} + 6\right) + \frac{3}{7} = 6 + \left(\frac{3}{7} + \frac{2}{5}\right)$ D. $\left(\frac{1}{8} + 2\right) + \frac{2}{3} = 2\left(\frac{1}{8} + \frac{2}{3}\right)$

55) What is x if $\sqrt{x - 15} = 7$?

    A. 46   C. 75

    B. 64   D. 81

56) If x is an odd integer and $5 < x < 9$, what is x?

    A. 8   C. 6

    B. 9   D. 7

57) The number that is 12 more than 113 is the cube of what number?

    A. 5   C. 15

    B. 9   D. 24

58) The measure of angle x is?

    A. $45°$

    B. $95°$

    C. $106°$

    D. $138°$

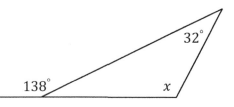

59) How many integers are between $\frac{13}{5}$ and 6.4?

    A. 1   C. 5

    B. 2   D. 7

60) Which of the following is a perfect square?

    A. 50   C. 112

    B. 91   D. 169

61) If $a + 8 = b + 14$, then?

    A. $a = b$ C. $a > b + 7$

    B. $a = 1$ D. $a - b > 0$

62) What is the volume of a cube with sides of 5 in?

    A. $27\ in^3$ C. $81\ in^3$

    B. $49\ in^3$ D. $125\ in^3$

63) What fraction of the following figure is shaded? (all triangles are equal)

    A. $\dfrac{1}{2}$

    B. $\dfrac{1}{3}$

    C. $\dfrac{3}{5}$

    D. $\dfrac{3}{4}$

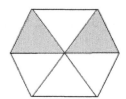

64) The ratio of two numbers is $3:2$. The sum of the two numbers is 45. What is the smaller of the two numbers?

A. 15

B. 18

C. 21

D. 28

STOP: This is the End of Test 4.

HSPT Mathematics Practice Test 5

2020 - 2021

Total number of questions: 64

Total time for two parts: 45 Minutes

Calculators are not allowed for this test.

HSPT Mathematics Practice Test Answer Sheet

Remove (or photocopy) this answer sheet and use it to complete the practice test.

HSPT Mathematics Practice Test 5 Answer Sheet		
1 Ⓐ Ⓑ Ⓒ Ⓓ	26 Ⓐ Ⓑ Ⓒ Ⓓ	51 Ⓐ Ⓑ Ⓒ Ⓓ
2 Ⓐ Ⓑ Ⓒ Ⓓ	27 Ⓐ Ⓑ Ⓒ Ⓓ	52 Ⓐ Ⓑ Ⓒ Ⓓ
3 Ⓐ Ⓑ Ⓒ Ⓓ	28 Ⓐ Ⓑ Ⓒ Ⓓ	53 Ⓐ Ⓑ Ⓒ Ⓓ
4 Ⓐ Ⓑ Ⓒ Ⓓ	29 Ⓐ Ⓑ Ⓒ Ⓓ	54 Ⓐ Ⓑ Ⓒ Ⓓ
5 Ⓐ Ⓑ Ⓒ Ⓓ	30 Ⓐ Ⓑ Ⓒ Ⓓ	55 Ⓐ Ⓑ Ⓒ Ⓓ
6 Ⓐ Ⓑ Ⓒ Ⓓ	31 Ⓐ Ⓑ Ⓒ Ⓓ	56 Ⓐ Ⓑ Ⓒ Ⓓ
7 Ⓐ Ⓑ Ⓒ Ⓓ	32 Ⓐ Ⓑ Ⓒ Ⓓ	57 Ⓐ Ⓑ Ⓒ Ⓓ
8 Ⓐ Ⓑ Ⓒ Ⓓ	33 Ⓐ Ⓑ Ⓒ Ⓓ	58 Ⓐ Ⓑ Ⓒ Ⓓ
9 Ⓐ Ⓑ Ⓒ Ⓓ	34 Ⓐ Ⓑ Ⓒ Ⓓ	59 Ⓐ Ⓑ Ⓒ Ⓓ
10 Ⓐ Ⓑ Ⓒ Ⓓ	35 Ⓐ Ⓑ Ⓒ Ⓓ	60 Ⓐ Ⓑ Ⓒ Ⓓ
11 Ⓐ Ⓑ Ⓒ Ⓓ	36 Ⓐ Ⓑ Ⓒ Ⓓ	61 Ⓐ Ⓑ Ⓒ Ⓓ
12 Ⓐ Ⓑ Ⓒ Ⓓ	37 Ⓐ Ⓑ Ⓒ Ⓓ	62 Ⓐ Ⓑ Ⓒ Ⓓ
13 Ⓐ Ⓑ Ⓒ Ⓓ	38 Ⓐ Ⓑ Ⓒ Ⓓ	63 Ⓐ Ⓑ Ⓒ Ⓓ
14 Ⓐ Ⓑ Ⓒ Ⓓ	39 Ⓐ Ⓑ Ⓒ Ⓓ	64 Ⓐ Ⓑ Ⓒ Ⓓ
15 Ⓐ Ⓑ Ⓒ Ⓓ	40 Ⓐ Ⓑ Ⓒ Ⓓ	
16 Ⓐ Ⓑ Ⓒ Ⓓ	41 Ⓐ Ⓑ Ⓒ Ⓓ	
17 Ⓐ Ⓑ Ⓒ Ⓓ	42 Ⓐ Ⓑ Ⓒ Ⓓ	
18 Ⓐ Ⓑ Ⓒ Ⓓ	43 Ⓐ Ⓑ Ⓒ Ⓓ	
19 Ⓐ Ⓑ Ⓒ Ⓓ	44 Ⓐ Ⓑ Ⓒ Ⓓ	
20 Ⓐ Ⓑ Ⓒ Ⓓ	45 Ⓐ Ⓑ Ⓒ Ⓓ	
21 Ⓐ Ⓑ Ⓒ Ⓓ	46 Ⓐ Ⓑ Ⓒ Ⓓ	
22 Ⓐ Ⓑ Ⓒ Ⓓ	47 Ⓐ Ⓑ Ⓒ Ⓓ	
23 Ⓐ Ⓑ Ⓒ Ⓓ	48 Ⓐ Ⓑ Ⓒ Ⓓ	
24 Ⓐ Ⓑ Ⓒ Ⓓ	49 Ⓐ Ⓑ Ⓒ Ⓓ	
25 Ⓐ Ⓑ Ⓒ Ⓓ	50 Ⓐ Ⓑ Ⓒ Ⓓ	

1) Simplify: $\frac{4\frac{3}{9}}{2\frac{1}{6}}$.

   A. 2

   B. $2\frac{1}{4}$

   C. 6

   D. $\frac{6}{11}$

2) If the rate is $2.15 per $100, how much tax must be paid on a car assessed at $18,000?

   A. $381.40

   B. $383

   C. $385.50

   D. $387

3) What number is 10 less than 40% of 70?

   A. 7

   B. 15

   C. 18

   D. 26

4) How many millimeters are in 1 meter?

   A. 0.1

   B. 10

   C. 100

   D. 1,000

5) A store offered a 15% discount off the regular price of a desk. The amount of the discount is $6. What is the regular price of the desk?

   A. $35

   B. $40

   C. $45

   D. $50

6) What value of x makes this equation true? $5x - 53 = 22$

   A. 11

   B. 15

   C. 19

   D.27

7) The figure below shows 2 circles. Points $D, E, F,$ and G are on line segment DG. The line segment DG is the diameter of the bigger circle and EF is the diameter of the smaller circle. The diameter of the larger circle is 17 mm? What is the radius of the smaller circle?

   A. 3 mm

   B. 4 mm

   C. 5 mm

   D. 6 mm

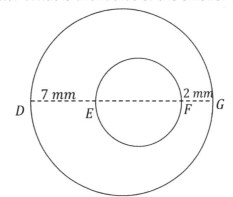

8) $(8 + 4^2) \div (18 \div 3) =$ ___

   A. 20   C. 4

   B. $\dfrac{1}{4}$ D. 6

9) What is the median of these numbers? 5, 10, 14, 9, 19, 6 16

   A. 9   C. 14

   B. 10   D. 16

10) Wood and glass make up 85% of a sculpture. If g represents the percentage of the sculpture that is made of glass, which equation can be used to find w, the percentage of the sculpture that is made of wood?

   A. $w = 100 - g$ C. $w = 100 - 85 - g$

   B. $w = \dfrac{g}{100}$ D. $w = 85 - g$

11) At a Zoo, the ratio of lions to tigers is 12 to 4. Which of the following could NOT be the total number of lions and tigers in the Zoo?

   A. 32   C. 98

   B. 64   D. 112

12) At noon, the temperature was 15 degrees. By midnight, it had dropped another 25 degrees. What was the temperature at midnight?

   A. 5 degrees above zero   C. 10 degrees above zero

   B. 5 degrees below zero   D. 10 degrees below zero

13) John is driving to visit his mother, who lives 480 miles away. How long will the drive be if John drives at an average speed of 40 mph?

   A. 95 minutes   C. 645 minutes

   B. 260 minutes   D. 720 minutes

14) $8(a - 3) = 16$, what is the value of a?

   A. 2   C. 7

   B. 5   D. 11

15) In a basket, there are equal numbers of red, white, yellow, and purple cards. Which of the following could be the number of cards in the basket?

    A. 123   C. 66

    B. 82   D. 56

16) If $3^{24} = 3^8 \times 3^x$, what is the value of x?

    A. 2   C. 3

    B. 1.5   D. 16

17) From last year, the price of gasoline has increased from $1.40 per gallon to $1.75 per gallon. The new price is what percent of the original price?

    A. 72%   C. 125%

    B. 115%   D. 160%

18) The eighth root of 256 is:

    A. 6   C. 8

    B. 4   D. 2

19) What is the value of $\sqrt{81} \times \sqrt{64}$?

    A. 56   C. 72

    B. $\sqrt{145}$ D. $\sqrt{18}$

20) Julie gives 6 pieces of candy to each of her friends. If Julie gives all her candy away, which amount of candy could have been the amount she distributed?

    A. 180   C. 243

    B. 217   D. 263

21) A circle has a diameter of 18 inches. What is its approximate area? ($\pi = 3.14$)

    A. 245.34   C. 84.00

    B. 145.44   D. 16.34

22) If $a = 4$, what is the value of b in this equation?

$$b = \frac{a^2}{4} + 2$$

    A. 10   C. 6

    B. 8   D. 4

23) Which of the following is an obtuse angle?

　　A. $129°$　　　　　　　　　　C. $78°$

　　B. $85°$　　　　　　　　　　D. $25°$

24) What is the sum of the prime numbers in the following list of numbers?

$$8, 14, 11, 18, 13, 22, 19, 42, 48$$

　　A. 32　　　　　　　　　　C. 43

　　B. 37　　　　　　　　　　D. 32

25) When 105 is divided by 6, the remainder is the same as when 87 is divided by

　　A. 8　　　　　　　　　　C. 5

　　B. 6　　　　　　　　　　D. 3

26) A square has an area of $81\ cm^2$. What is its perimeter?

　　A. $28\ cm$　　　　　　　　C. $34\ cm^2$

　　B. $32\ cm^2$　　　　　　　D. $36\ cm$

27) The cube root of 3,375 is?

　　A. 12　　　　　　　　　　C. 75

　　B. 15　　　　　　　　　　D. 186

28) How many $\frac{1}{6}$ cup servings are in a package of cheese that contains $5\frac{1}{2}$ cups altogether?

　　A. 20　　　　　　　　　　C. 24

　　B. 22　　　　　　　　　　D. 33

29) Find the slope of the line running through the points $(6, 7)$ and $(5, 3)$.

　　A. $\dfrac{1}{4}$　　　　　　　　　C. -4

　　B. 4　　　　　　　　　　D. $-\dfrac{1}{4}$

30) Ella buys five items costing $3.26, $15.69, $2.50, $4.66, and $17.99. What is the estimated total cost of Ella's items?

　　A. between $25 and $30　　　　C. between $35 and $40

　　B. between $30 and $35　　　　D. between $42 and $47

31) Which statement about the number 749,382.16 is true

   A. The digit 6 has a value of (6×100)

   B. The digit 4 has a value of (4×100)

   C. The digit 8 has a value of (8×10)

   D. The digit 9 has a value of (9×100)

32) Simplify: $3(4x^5)^3$.

   A. $12x^{15}$ C. $12x^8$

   B. $192x^{15}$ D. $192x^8$

33) If N is an even number, which of the following is always an odd number?

   A. $\frac{N}{2}$ C. $2N$

   B. $N + 4$ D. $N + 1$

34) Four people can paint 4 houses in 10 days. How many people are needed to paint 8 houses in 5 days?

   A. 8   C. 13

   B. 9   D. 16

35) Emma draws a shape on her paper. The shape has four sides. It has only one pair of parallel sides. What shape does Emma draw?

   A. Parallelogram   C. Square

   B. Rectangle   D. Trapezoid

36) Jack ordered 19 pizzas. Each pizza has 8 slices. How many slices of pizza did Jack ordered ?

   A. 124   C. 156

   B. 152   D. 180

37) In the following figure, MN is $32\ cm$. How long is ON?

   A. $24\ cm$
   B. $18\ cm$
   C. $16\ cm$
   D. $4\ cm$

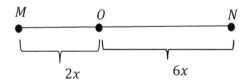

38) A barista averages making 18 coffees per hour. At this rate, how many hours will it take until she's made 1,800 coffees?

A. 95 hours

C. 100 hours

B. 90 hours

D. 105 hours

39) In the figure below, what is the value of x?

A. 10 cm

B. 12 cm

C. 14 cm

D. 16 cm

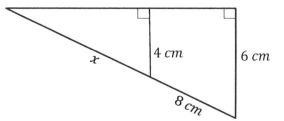

40) A bank is offering 4.5% simple interest on a savings account. If you deposit $8,000, how much interest will you earn in five years?

A. $360

C. $1,800

B. $720

D. $3,600

41) Which of the following could be the product of two consecutive prime numbers?

A. 2

C. 14

B. 10

D. 15

42) Which of the following lists shows the fractions in order from least to greatest?

$$\frac{3}{4}, \frac{1}{7}, \frac{3}{8}, \frac{5}{11}$$

A. $\frac{3}{8}, \frac{1}{7}, \frac{3}{4}, \frac{5}{11}$

C. $\frac{1}{7}, \frac{3}{8}, \frac{5}{11}, \frac{3}{4}$

B. $\frac{1}{7}, \frac{5}{11}, \frac{3}{8}, \frac{3}{4}$

D. $\frac{3}{8}, \frac{1}{7}, \frac{5}{11}, \frac{3}{4}$

43) The average of five consecutive numbers is 38. What is the smallest number?

A. 38

C. 34

B. 36

D. 12

44) In the triangle below, if the measure of angle A is 37 degrees, then what is the value of y? (figure is NOT drawn to scale)

A. 62

B. 70

C. 78

D. 86

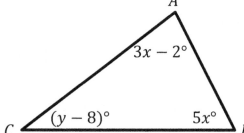

45) What is the value of $4! \times 5$?

    A. 480   C. 180

    B. 240   D. 120

46) The supervisor of a small company is designing a new open office layout and thinks that employees will need 8 chairs for every 4 desks. How many office chairs will be needed for an office building with 50 desks?

    A. 40 chairs   C. 80 chairs

    B. 60 chairs   D. 100 chairs

47) How many square feet of tile is needed for a 14 feet $\times$ 14 feet room?

    A. 196 square feet   C. 105 square feet

    B. 113.5 square feet   D. 50 square feet

48) If $2y + 4y + 2y = -24$, then what is the value of y?

    A. -3 C. -1

    B. -2 D. 0

49) There are 150 rooms that need to be painted and only 8 painters available. If there are still 30 rooms unpainted by the end of the day, what is the average number of rooms that each painter has painted?

    A. 15   C. 20

    B. 18   D. 22

50) $\dfrac{1}{6b^2} + \dfrac{1}{6b} = \dfrac{1}{b^2}$, then $b = $?

    A. $-\dfrac{16}{15}$ C. $-\dfrac{15}{16}$

    B. 5   D. 8

51) The square of a number is $\dfrac{36}{64}$. What is the cube of that number?

    A. $\dfrac{6}{8}$ C. $\dfrac{216}{512}$

    B. $\dfrac{25}{254}$ D. $\dfrac{125}{64}$

52) What is the distance between the points $(1, 3)$ and $(-2, 7)$?

A. 3

C. 5

B. 4

D. 6

53) Which is not a prime number?

A. 181

C. 131

B. 151

D. 122

54) Will has been working on a report for 4 hours each day, 7 days a week for 2 weeks. How many minutes has will worked on his report?

A. 5,360 minutes

C. 3,360 minutes

B. 4,444 minutes

D. 1,680 minutes

55) $x^2 - 49 = 0$, x could be:

A. 6

C. 12

B. 7

D. 15

56) In the following right triangle, what is the value of x rounded to the nearest hundredth?

A. 5

B. 6

C. 8

D. 10

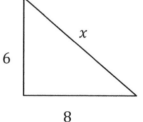

57) The average of $14, 16, 21$ and x is 20. What is the value of x?

A. 29

C. 22

B. 14

D. 4

58) 25 is What percent of 50?

A. 50%

C. 5%

B. 25%

D. 150%

59) Which of the following points lies on the line $x + 2y = 4$?

A. $(-2, 3)$

C. $(-1, 3)$

B. $(1, 2)$

D. $(-3, 4)$

60) If $2x - 6 = 4.5$, What is the value of $8x - 2$?

    A. 12

    B. 16.50

    C. 32.25

    D. 40

61) What is the value of x in the following figure?

    A. 160

    B. 145

    C. 125

    D. 105

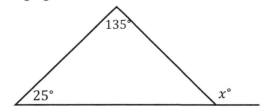

62) The perimeter of a rectangular yard is 66 meters. What is its length if its width is twice its length?

    A. 11 meters

    B. 18 meters

    C. 20 meters

    D. 25 meters

63) Two dice are thrown simultaneously, what is the probability of getting a sum of 6 or 9?

    A. $\dfrac{1}{3}$

    B. $\dfrac{1}{4}$

    C. $\dfrac{1}{6}$

    D. $\dfrac{1}{12}$

64) What's the square root of $16x^2$?

    A. $4\sqrt{x}$

    B. $16x$

    C. $4x$

    D. $\sqrt{4x}$

STOP: This is the End of Test 5.

HSPT Mathematics Practice Tests Answer Keys

Now, it's time to review your results to see where you went wrong and what areas you need to improve.

HSPT Practice Test 1 Answers

1-	C	17-	A	33-	A	49-	A
2-	D	18-	C	34-	C	50-	D
3-	A	19-	A	35-	A	51-	C
4-	B	20-	A	36-	C	52-	C
5-	D	21-	C	37-	A	53-	B
6-	C	22-	C	38-	B	54-	D
7-	D	23-	B	39-	B	55-	C
8-	A	24-	A	40-	C	56-	D
9-	A	25-	C	41-	A	57-	B
10-	C	26-	C	42-	D	58-	C
11-	A	27-	B	43-	D	59-	C
12-	A	28-	C	44-	B	60-	D
13-	A	29-	A	45-	B	61-	C
14-	B	30-	D	46-	C	62-	A
15-	A	31-	C	47-	A	63-	A
16-	C	32-	D	48-	D	64-	C

HSPT Practice Test 2 Answers

1-	B	17-	A	33-	A	49-	C
2-	D	18-	C	34-	B	50-	A
3-	C	19-	D	35-	A	51-	C
4-	B	20-	C	36-	B	52-	C
5-	D	21-	B	37-	B	53-	C
6-	A	22-	D	38-	A	54-	B
7-	B	23-	A	39-	A	55-	D
8-	B	24-	B	40-	D	56-	D
9-	A	25-	D	41-	B	57-	D
10-	B	26-	A	42-	B	58-	A
11-	C	27-	C	43-	D	59-	C
12-	A	28-	D	44-	D	60-	A
13-	C	29-	B	45-	D	61-	C
14-	A	30-	D	46-	D	62-	D
15-	C	31-	D	47-	C	63-	C
16-	B	32-	D	48-	C	64-	A

HSPT Mathematics Practice Test 3 Answers

1-	**A**	17-	**C**	33-	**A**	49-	**B**
2-	**A**	18-	**A**	34-	**A**	50-	**C**
3-	**D**	19-	**D**	35-	**B**	51-	**B**
4-	**B**	20-	**A**	36-	**B**	52-	**C**
5-	**B**	21-	**D**	37-	**B**	53-	**A**
6-	**C**	22-	**C**	38-	**A**	54-	**C**
7-	**D**	23-	**C**	39-	**B**	55-	**B**
8-	**C**	24-	**A**	40-	**C**	56-	**B**
9-	**C**	25-	**A**	41-	**D**	57-	**B**
10-	**D**	26-	**C**	42-	**B**	58-	**D**
11-	**A**	27-	**B**	43-	**C**	59-	**A**
12-	**A**	28-	**A**	44-	**D**	60-	**A**
13-	**B**	29-	**C**	45-	**D**	61-	**D**
14-	**C**	30-	**B**	46-	**D**	62-	**B**
15-	**C**	31-	**C**	47-	**B**	63-	**C**
16-	**B**	32-	**D**	48-	**B**	64-	**B**

HSPT Mathematics Practice Test 4 Answers

1-	D	17-	A	33-	C	49-	B
2-	D	18-	D	34-	D	50-	C
3-	B	19-	C	35-	B	51-	B
4-	A	20-	B	36-	C	52-	C
5-	A	21-	A	37-	D	53-	B
6-	B	22-	A	38-	C	54-	B
7-	D	23-	B	39-	B	55-	B
8-	C	24-	A	40-	B	56-	D
9-	D	25-	B	41-	A	57-	A
10-	A	26-	D	42-	D	58-	C
11-	A	27-	A	43-	C	59-	C
12-	A	28-	B	44-	C	60-	D
13-	D	29-	C	45-	B	61-	D
14-	A	30-	B	46-	C	62-	D
15-	C	31-	A	47-	B	63-	B
16-	C	32-	B	48-	C	64-	B

HSPT Mathematics Practice Test 5 Answers

1-	A	17-	C	33-	D	49-	A
2-	D	18-	D	34-	D	50-	B
3-	C	19-	C	35-	D	51-	C
4-	D	20-	A	36-	B	52-	C
5-	B	21-	A	37-	A	53-	D
6-	B	22-	C	38-	C	54-	C
7-	B	23-	A	39-	D	55-	B
8-	C	24-	C	40-	C	56-	D
9-	B	25-	D	41-	D	57-	A
10-	D	26-	D	42-	C	58-	A
11-	C	27-	B	43-	B	59-	A
12-	D	28-	D	44-	D	60-	D
13-	D	29-	B	45-	D	61-	A
14-	B	30-	D	46-	D	62-	A
15-	D	31-	C	47-	A	63-	D
16-	D	32-	B	48-	A	64-	C

HSPT Mathematics Practice Tests

Answers and Explanations

HSPT Mathematics Practice Test 1

1) Choice C is correct

Use Exponent's rules: $x^a \times x^b = x^{a+b} \rightarrow (x^5).(x^4) = x^{5+4} = x^9$

2) Choice D is correct

Line up the numbers:
$$\begin{array}{r} 0.79 \\ + 7.65 \\ 6.24 \\ \hline 14.68 \end{array}$$

3) Choice A is correct

A. 7 is a prime number.

B. 14 is not a prime number. It is divisible by 2.

C. 21 is not a prime number. It is divisible by 3.

D. 35 is not a prime number. It is divisible by 5.

4) Choice B is correct

$x + y = M$, $x = 14$, then: $14 + y = M$

$y = M - 14$, then: $2y = 2(M - 14)$

5) Choice D is correct

Circumference $= d\pi \Rightarrow C = 5.4\pi = 16.956 \approx 17$ inches

6) Choice C is correct

$$\frac{1}{x} = \frac{1}{\frac{4}{3}} = \frac{\frac{1}{1}}{\frac{4}{3}} = \frac{3}{4}$$

7) Choice D is correct

Choice D represents the given information. $E = 4 + A, A = S - 3$

8) Choice A is correct

$18a + 20 = 38 \rightarrow 18a = 38 - 20 \rightarrow 18a = 18 \rightarrow a = 1$

9) Choice A is correct

$\frac{2^4}{x} = \frac{2^4}{4} = \frac{16}{4} = 4$

10) Choice C is correct

$250 + 45 = 295$

11) Choice A is correct

$10x - 5 = 35 \rightarrow 10x = 40 \rightarrow x = \frac{40}{10} = 4$

12) Choice A is correct

A. $\frac{23}{3} = 7.66$, B. $\frac{24}{3} = 8$, C. $\frac{12}{3} = 4$, D. $\frac{27}{3} = 9$

13) Choice A is correct

Area of a rectangle $= width \times length = 35 \times 45 = 1,575$

14) Choice B is correct

Find the value of each choice:

A. $2 \times 2 \times 5 \times 5 = 100$

B. $2 \times 2 \times 2 \times 2 \times 5 \times 5 = 400$

C. $2 \times 5 = 10$

D. $2 \times 2 \times 2 \times 5 \times 5 = 200$

15) Choice A is correct

$180 \div 15 = 12$

16) Choice C is correct

$(11 + 7) \div (3^3 \div 3) = (18) \div (27 \div 3) = (18) \div (9) = 2$

17) Choice A is correct

$\{21, 18, 15, 12, 9\}$

18) Choice C is correct

$2x + 12 = 2(-3) + 12 = -6 + 12 = 6$

19) Choice A is correct

$8 < x \leq 10$, then cannot be equal to 8

20) Choice A is correct

$x + y = 14$

$8x + 8y \rightarrow 8(x + y) \rightarrow 14 \times 8 = 112$

21) Choice C is correct

$5 + x \geq 18 \rightarrow x \geq 18 - 5 \rightarrow x \geq 13$

22) Choice C is correct

$\frac{25}{100} \times 350 = x \, , \, x = \frac{25 \times 350}{100} = 87.5$

23) Choice B is correct

$\frac{18 + 14 + 5 + 24 + 24}{5} = \frac{85}{5} = 17$

24) Choice A is correct

$\{2, 4, 8, 14, 22\}$

25) Choice C is correct

$0.14 \times 100 = 14\%$

26) Choice C is correct

$\frac{14}{28} = \frac{1}{2}$

27) Choice B is correct

$\frac{14}{25} = 0.56$

28) Choice C is correct

$8 + x = 5 \rightarrow x = 5 - 8 \rightarrow x = -3$

29) Choice A is correct

$\sqrt{36} = 6$

30) Choice D is correct

$3 \times 3 \times 3 \times 3 \times 3 = 243$

31) Choice C is correct

A. $\frac{3}{4} = 0.75$, B. $\frac{2}{5} = 0.4$, C. $\frac{8}{9} \approx 0.88$, D. $\frac{2}{3} \approx 0.66$

Choice C $\left(\frac{8}{9}\right)$ is the largest number in the choices.

32) Choice D is correct

1 quart = 0.25 gallon. 36 quarts = $36 \times 0.25 = 9$ gallons. Then: $\frac{9}{2} = 4.5$ weeks

33) Choice A is correct

$-7a = 49 \rightarrow a = \frac{49}{-7} = -7$

34) Choice C is correct

$x^2 + 5x - 6 = (x + 6)(x - 1)$

35) Choice A is correct

$136 \times 45 = 6,120$

36) Choice C is correct

$2ABC = 2(6)(4)(5) = 240$

37) Choice A is correct

$$\frac{8}{1} = \frac{152}{x} \rightarrow x = \frac{152}{8} = 19$$

38) Choice B is correct

The area of the non-shaded region is equal to the area of the bigger rectangle subtracted by the area of smaller rectangle.

Area of the bigger rectangle $= 12 \times 16 = 192$

Area of the smaller rectangle $= 10 \times 4 = 40$

Area of the non-shaded region $= 192 - 40 = 152$

39) Choice B is correct

$160 - 73 = 87$

40) Choice C is correct

$$\frac{24}{10} = 2.4$$

41) Choice A is correct

9,823.3

42) Choice D is correct

$$\sqrt[3]{216} = \sqrt[3]{6^3} = 6$$

43) Choice D is correct

$6x^2 + 5x - 13 = 6(6)^2 + 5(6) - 13 = 233$

44) Choice B is correct

A. $y = 1 - x \rightarrow y = 1 - (-1) = 2$

B. $y = x + 1 \rightarrow y = (-1) + 1 = 0$ This cannot be the equation of line l

C. $x = -1 \rightarrow (-1) = -1$

D. $y = x + 3 \rightarrow y = (-1) + 3 = 2$

45) Choice B is correct

$$C = 2\pi r \rightarrow 35 = 2\pi r \rightarrow r = \frac{35}{2\pi} = 5.57 \cong 5.6$$

46) Choice C is correct

$$\frac{8}{12} + \frac{4}{3} + \frac{2}{6} = \frac{8 + 4(4) + 2(2)}{12} = \frac{28}{12} = \frac{7}{3} = 2\frac{1}{3}$$

47) Choice A is correct

$$\frac{8}{10} = 0.8$$

48) Choice D is correct

$$5! = 5 \times 4 \times 3 \times 2 \times 1$$

49) Choice A is correct

Set proportion: $\frac{360}{x} = \frac{90}{1} \rightarrow 90x = 360 \rightarrow x = 4$

50) Choice D is correct

Since Julie gives 8 pieces of candy to each of her friends, then number of pieces of candies must be divisible by 8.

A. $187 \div 8 = 23.375$

B. $223 \div 8 = 27.875$

C. $343 \div 8 = 42.875$

D. $232 \div 8 = 29$

Only choice D gives a whole number.

51) Choice C is correct

$$9x + 12 - (9x - 3) = 9x + 12 - 9x + 3 = 12 + 3 = 15$$

52) Choice C is correct

$$140 + 20 + 8 = 168$$

53) Choice B is correct

$(x + 4)(x + 3) = x^2 + 3x + 4x + 12 = x^2 + 7x + 12$

54) Choice D is correct

Perimeter of a triangle $= side\ 1 + side\ 2 + side\ 3 = 35 + 35 + 35 = 105$

55) Choice C is correct

Let's review the choices provided. Put the values of x and y in the equation.

A. $(1, 2) \rightarrow x = 1 \rightarrow y = 5(1) - 3 = 2$ This is true!

B. $(-2, -13) \rightarrow x = -2 \rightarrow y = 5(-2) - 3 = -13$ This is true!

C. $(3, 18) \rightarrow x = 3 \rightarrow y = 5(3) - 3 = 12$ This is not true!

D. $(2, 7) \rightarrow x = 2 \rightarrow y = 5(2) - 3 = 7$ This is true!

56) Choice D is correct

$1 - (-8) = 1 + 8 = 9$

57) Choice B is correct

$x^2 - 64 = 0 \rightarrow x^2 = 64 \rightarrow x = 8$

58) Choice C is correct

$(x^8)^3 = x^{24}$

59) Choice C is correct

Angle a and the angle 145 degrees are equal. $a = 145°$

60) Choice D is correct

$P = 2(x + y), A = x . y$

$P = 2(x + y) \rightarrow 112 = 2(22 + y) \rightarrow 112 = 44 + 2y \rightarrow 68 = 2y \rightarrow y = 34$

$A = 22 \times 34 = 748$

61) Choice C is correct

$\sqrt{25} \times \sqrt{36} = 5 \times 6 = 30$

62) Choice A is correct

$7 \times 7 \times 7 = 343$

63) Choice A is correct

The angles on a straight line add up to 180 degrees. Then:

$x + 25 + y + 2x + y = 180$

Then, $3x + 2y = 180 - 25 \rightarrow 3x + 2y = 155 \rightarrow 3(35) + 2y = 155$

$\rightarrow 2y = 155 - 105 = 50 \rightarrow y = 25$

64) Choice C is correct

The factors of 15 are: $\{ 1, 3, 5, 15 \}$. The factors of 25 are: $\{ 1, 5, 25 \}$. Then: $GCF = 5$

HSPT Mathematics Practice Test 2

1)   Choice B is correct

$\frac{6^6}{6} = 6^5 = 7,776$

2)   Choice D is correct

$8a - 15 = 9 \rightarrow 8a = 9 + 15 \rightarrow 8a = 24 \rightarrow a = 3$

3)   Choice C is correct

Let x be the original price. Then:

$\$1,912.50 = x - 0.15(x) \rightarrow 1,912.50 = 0.85x \rightarrow x = \dfrac{1,912.50}{0.85} \rightarrow x = 2,250.00$

4)   Choice B is correct

$\dfrac{(11\ feet + 7\ yards)}{4} = \dfrac{(11\ feet + 21\ feet\ )}{4} = \dfrac{(32\ feet\ )}{4} = 8$ feet

5)   Choice D is correct

Let x be total number of cards in the box, then number of red cards is: $x - 246$

The probability of choosing a red card is one third. Then:

Probability $= \dfrac{1}{3} = \dfrac{x - 246}{x}$

Use cross multiplication to solve for x.

$x \times 1 = 3(x - 246) \rightarrow x = 3x - 738 \rightarrow 2x = 738 \rightarrow x = 369$

6) Choice A is correct

Simplify and combine like terms.

$(6x^3 - 8x^2 + 2x^4) - (4x^2 - 2x^4 + 2x^3) \rightarrow (6x^3 - 8x^2 + 2x^4) - 4x^2 + 2x^4 - 2x^3$

$\rightarrow 4x^4 + 4x^3 - 12x^2$

7) Choice B is correct

Write a proportion and solve for x: $\frac{1}{S} = \frac{x}{20}$

Solving for variable, x: $Sx = 20 \rightarrow x = \frac{20}{S}$. Emma can read $\frac{20}{S}$ pages, in 20 minutes

8) Choice B is correct

Sam can arrange $\frac{1}{2}$ of the storeroom in 1 hour. Jim can arrange $\frac{1}{3}$ of the storeroom in 1 hour.

When working together, the following equation may be written: $\frac{1}{2}x + \frac{1}{3}x = 1$

Solve for x: $\frac{3x+2x}{6} = 1 \rightarrow \frac{5x}{6} = 1 \rightarrow 5x = 6 \rightarrow x = \frac{6}{5} = 1.2 \rightarrow x = 1$ hour and 12 minutes.

9) Choice A is correct

The following proportion may be used to determine how much Jack will make next month:

$\frac{180}{540} = \frac{160}{x} \rightarrow 180x = 86,400 \rightarrow x = 480$

10) Choice B is correct

$\sqrt{5}$ has a decimal expansion that does not terminate or repeat ($\sqrt{5} = 2.23606789$). Thus, it is an irrational number.

11) Choice D is correct

Simple interest is represented by the formula, $I = Prt$

$3,000 = (8,500)(r)(6) \rightarrow 3,000 = 51,000r \rightarrow r = 0.0588$ or 6%

12) Choice A is correct

1 feet= 12 inches

8 feet, 10 inches = 106 inches, 5 feet, 12 inches = 72 inches

$106 + 72 = 178$

13) Choice C is correct

The absolute value of a number is the distance the number is from 0. The integer, -3 is 3 units from 0 on the number line. Thus, it has an absolute value of 3.

14) Choice A is correct

$(5.2 + 4.3 + 4.5)\, x = x$, $14x = x$, Then $x = 0$

15) Choice C is correct

9 hour = 540 minutes

$\frac{60}{1} = \frac{540}{x} \rightarrow x = \frac{540}{60} = 9$

16) Choice B is correct

A. $2^2 = 4 \neq 8$

B. $3^2 = 9$

C. $4^2 = 16 \neq 20$

D. $5^2 = 25 \neq 30$

17) Choice A is correct

$8.82 \div 2.4 = 3.675$

18) Choice C is correct

Aligning the decimals at the decimal point and adhering to the same integer addition computation properties, the sum is equal to:

$$22.07 + 0.035 + 14.3954 + 0.0005 + 20 = 56.5009$$

19) Choice D is correct

By first performing the computations within the parentheses, the expression may be rewritten as 3×11, which equals 33.

$$(12 \div 4) \times (17 - 6) = 3 \times 11 = 33$$

20) Choice C is correct

Since the two lines in the circle are perpendicular, then: $x = 12$

21) Choice B is correct

$160 < 8x < 240 \rightarrow \frac{160}{8} < x < \frac{240}{8} \rightarrow 20 < x < 30$, then, only choice B, 25, is correct.

22) Choice D is correct

The percentage, 58%, may be converted to a decimal by moving the decimal point two places to left. In other words, 58 is divided by 100, since one percent represents one-hundredth: $58\% = 58 \div 100 = 0.58$

23) Choice A is correct

Use PEMDAS (order of operation):

$$-20 + 6 \times (-5) - [4 + 22 \times (-4)] \div 2 = -20 - 30 - [4 - 88] \div 2 = -50 - [-84] \div 2$$
$$= -50 + 84 \div 2 = -50 + 42 = -8$$

24) Choice B is correct

The problem may be modeled by the following system of equations:

$M = P + 10$ and $M + P = 48$.

Substituting the expression for M, into the second equation, gives:

$$P + 10 + P = 48 \rightarrow 2P = 48 - 10 = 38 \rightarrow P = 19$$

Thus, there are 19 peaches. Since there are 48 peaches and mangoes in all, there must be 29 mangoes.

25) Choice D is correct

$$4z + 16 \rightarrow 4(-4) + 16 = 0$$

26) Choice A is correct

$$12a + 10 = 160 \rightarrow 12a = 160 - 10 \rightarrow 12a = 150 \rightarrow a = 12.5$$

27) Choice C is correct

$$35 \times 5 = 175$$

28) Choice D is correct

A. $\frac{38}{4} = 9.5$, B. $\frac{46}{4} = 11.5$, C. $\frac{85}{4} = 21.25$, D. $\frac{108}{4} = 27$

29) Choice B is correct

$$10^5 = 10 \times 10 \times 10 \times 10 \times 10 = 100,000$$

30) Choice D is correct

The figure shows 2 completely shaded squares, plus $\frac{3}{4}$. Thus, the figure represents the mixed number, $2\frac{3}{4}$.

31) Choice D is correct

$LCM = 36$

32) Choice D is correct

180 of $\frac{1}{6}$ pound paperback books together weigh 30 pounds.

33) Choice A is correct

Each worker can walk 3 dogs: $6 \div 3 = 2$

5 workers can walk 10 dogs. $5 \times 2 = 10$

34) Choice B is correct

The sum equals 0.80, which may also be written as $\frac{80}{100} = \frac{8}{10} = \frac{4}{5}$

35) Choice A is correct

$Emily = Daniel\ ,\ Emily = 5\ Claire$

$Daniel = 20 + Claire$

$Emily = Daniel \rightarrow Emily = 20 + Claire$

$Emily = 5\ Claire \rightarrow 5\ Claire = 20 + Claire \rightarrow 5\ Claire\ Claire = 20$

$4\ Claire = 20 \rightarrow Claire = 5$

36) Choice B is correct

$Speed = \frac{distance}{time}$

$69 = \frac{2,500}{time} \rightarrow time = \frac{2,500}{69} \approx 36.23$

37) Choice B is correct

$\frac{8}{40} = \frac{x}{150} \rightarrow x = \frac{8 \times 150}{40} = 30$

38) Choice A is correct

$\frac{1}{x} = \frac{\frac{1}{1}}{\frac{4}{7}} = \frac{7}{4}$

39) Choice A is correct

The square of the given fraction may be written as $\frac{4^2}{9^2}$ or $\frac{16}{81}$

40) Choice D is correct

The factors of 50 are: $\{1, 2, 5, 10, 25, 50\}$

41) Choice B is correct

2 is in the place value of thousandths in number 4.8325.

42) Choice B is correct

$0.542 > 0.0540$

43) Choice D is correct

The sum of the two negative integers is a negative number.

$(-25) + (-12) = -25 - 12 = -37$

44) Choice D is correct

$68 - 25 = 43$

45) Choice D is correct

Moving the decimal to the right of the 5 gives 5.61×10^{-4}, since the decimal must be moved 4 places to right.

46) Choice D is correct

Digit 3 and 6 end in the hundredths place. This means $0.36 = \frac{36}{100}$. When simplified to simplest form, $\frac{36}{100} = \frac{9}{25}$

47) Choice C is correct

The correct graph should show one ray, with a closed point on the integer -1, which points to the left, and another ray, with a closed point on the integer, 2, which points to the right.

48) Choice C is correct

Divide 1 by 9 children. The answer is $\frac{1}{9}$

49) Choice C is correct

The amount he will need for 4 cakes is equal to the product of $2\frac{1}{4}$ and 4: $2\frac{1}{4} \times 4 = \frac{9}{4} \times 4 = 9$

50) Choice A is correct

$\frac{4}{10} = \frac{x}{5} \rightarrow x = \frac{4 \times 5}{10} = 2$

51) Choice C is correct

$\frac{19}{10} = 1.9$

52) Choice C is correct

The original price of the chair may be found by solving the equation, $0.20x = 30$. Thus, $x = 150$. Since she saves $30, she pays $30 less or $150 - $30 = $120

53) Choice C is correct

$\frac{5}{4} = 1.25$

54) Choice B is correct

$7 \times 7 \times 7 \times 7 \times 7 = 7^5$

55) Choice D is correct

$\frac{1}{3}$ of the distance is $5\frac{1}{4}$ miles. Then: $\frac{1}{3} \times 5\frac{1}{4} = \frac{1}{3} \times \frac{21}{4} = \frac{21}{12}$

Converting $\frac{21}{12}$ to a mixed number gives: $\frac{21}{12} = 1\frac{9}{12} = 1\frac{3}{4}$

56) Choice D is correct

$$2\frac{2}{3} - 1\frac{5}{6} = 2\frac{4}{6} - 1\frac{5}{6} = \frac{16}{6} - \frac{11}{6} = \frac{5}{6}$$

57) Choice D is correct

$$\frac{4lab}{5} = \frac{4(3)(5)(3)}{5} = 36$$

58) Choice A is correct

Use interest rate formula: $Interest = principal \times rate \times time = 1{,}300 \times 0.05 \times 2 = 130$

59) Choice C is correct

y is the intersection of the three circles. Therefore, it must be odd (from circle A), negative (from circle B), and multiple of 5 (from circle C).

From the choices, only -5 is odd, negative and multiple of 5.

60) Choice A is correct

Charlotte $= 48$, Charlotte $= 2$ Avery, Avery $= \frac{48}{2} = 24$

61) Choice C is correct

$$A = \frac{1}{2}bh \rightarrow A = \frac{1}{2}(28)(8) = 112$$

62) Choice D is correct

$$180° - 55° = 125° \rightarrow x = 125°$$

63) Choice C is correct

To find the number of possible outfit combinations, multiply number of options for each factor: $3 \times 5 \times 4 = 60$

64) Choice A is correct

Oven 1 $= 4$ oven 2

If Oven 2 burns 3 then oven 1 burns 12 pizzas. $3 + 12 = 15$

HSPT Mathematics Practice Test 3

1)   Choice A is correct

Simple interest is represented by the formula, $I = prt = (5,000)(0.04)(6) = 1,200$

2)   Choice A is correct

$$\frac{2^3}{x-2} = \frac{2^3}{4-2} = \frac{8}{2} = 4$$

3)   Choice D is correct

The average is equal to the ratio of the amount spent to the number of days in a week. Thus, the average maybe written as $\frac{35}{7} = 5$. he spent an average of 5 per day.

4)   Choice B is correct

$0.00832 \div 2 = 0.00416$

5)   Choice B is correct

$-45 + 6 - 12 = -51$

6)   Choice C is correct

When multiplying terms with the same base, the exponents should be added. Thus, $10^6 \times 10^3 = 10^9$

7)   Choice D is correct

The decimal will be moved to the right 5 places. Thus 3 zeros will be added to the right of 348, giving 348,000.

8)   Choice C is correct

Diameter $= 6 \rightarrow$ radius $= \frac{6}{2} = 3$

Area of the circle is: πr^2. Substituting 3 for r gives area $= \pi(3)^2 = 9\pi$

9) Choice C is correct

The problem may be modeled as $120x = 45$. Dividing both sides of equation by 120 gives $x = 0.375$ or 37.5%

10) Choice D is correct

There are 16 triangles. Eight of them are shaded. 8 out of 16 is $\frac{8}{16} = \frac{1}{2}$

11) Choice A is correct

Average$= \frac{sum}{total} = \frac{42+38+34}{3} = \frac{114}{3} = 38$

12) Choice A is correct

$AB = 12$ and $AC = 5$. $BC = \sqrt{12^2 + 5^2} = \sqrt{144 + 25} = \sqrt{169} = 13$

Perimeter $= 5 + 12 + 13 = 30$. Area $= \frac{5 \times 12}{2} = 5 \times 6 = 30$

In this case, the ratio of the perimeter of the triangle to its area is: $\frac{30}{30} = 1$

If the sides AB and AC become twice longer, then: $AB = 24$ And $AC = 10$

$BC = \sqrt{24^2 + 10^2} = \sqrt{576 + 100} = \sqrt{676} = 26$. Perimeter $= 26 + 24 + 10 = 60$

Area $= \frac{10 \times 24}{2} = 10 \times 12 = 120$

13) Choice B is correct

$|-6 + 7| = 1 \rightarrow |-1| = 1$

14) Choice C is correct

85% of 40 is: $85\% \ of \ 40 = 0.85 \times 40 = 34$. So, the student solves 34 questions correctly.

15) Choice C is correct

If $\frac{3}{5}$ are boys, so $\frac{2}{5}$ are girls. $\frac{2}{5}$ of 240 equals $\frac{2}{5} \times 240 = 96$

16) Choice B is correct

First find $\frac{1}{5}$ of 45: $\frac{1}{5} \times 45 = 9$. Then subtract: $9 - 8 = 1$

17) Choice C is correct

If $1\ cm = 90$ miles, then $\frac{1}{3}\ cm = 30$ miles. Therefore, $2\frac{1}{3}\ cm = 2(90) + 30 = 210$

18) Choice A is correct

Sum of the angles of a straight line is $180°$.

$48 + 22 + (x + 8) = 180 \rightarrow x + 78 = 180 \rightarrow x = 102$

19) Choice D is correct

Use the mean formula: $\dfrac{some\ of\ the\ values}{number\ of\ values} = \dfrac{5+3+14+22+12+6+1}{7} = \dfrac{63}{7} = 9$

$\frac{1}{3}$ of 9 is $\frac{1}{3} \times 9 = 3$

20) Choice A is correct

Figure out this problem with algebra: $\frac{2}{5}x = 4 \times 3 \rightarrow \frac{2}{5}x = 12 \rightarrow x = 12 \times \frac{5}{2} = 30$

21) Choice D is correct

The symbol ∩ stands for intersection. The intersection of two or more sets is the set of elements common to both sets. In this case, the common elements are 2 and 5.

22) Choice C is correct

$48 + x = 43 \rightarrow x = 43 - 48 \rightarrow x = -5$

23) Choice C is correct

Start with the operations in the parentheses first: $(-3)^4 = 81$

Then continue with the operations outside the parentheses: $4(-3)^4 = 4(81) = 324$

$1 + 4(-3)^4 = 1 + 324 = 325$

24) Choice A is correct

The reciprocal of a fraction is the fraction reversed. To find the answer, you would have to rename $2\frac{1}{5} = \frac{11}{5}$; $\frac{11}{5}$ is the reciprocal of $\frac{5}{11}$.

25) Choice A is correct

$13^2 = 169$ and $14^2 = 196$. The square root of 180 is between 13 and 14.

26) Choice C is correct

$(5 + 7) \div (3^2 \div 3) = (12) \div (3) = 4$

27) Choice B is correct

First convert mixed number to fraction, then rename the numbers with a common denominator: $\frac{27}{8} + 9 = \frac{27+72}{8} = \frac{99}{8} = 12\frac{3}{8}$

28) Choice A is correct

The sale price of the car is 90% of regular price. Thus, the following equation may be used to solve the problem: $18,000 = 0.90x \rightarrow x = 20,000$. Thus, the regular price of the car is $20,000

29) Choice C is correct

$180° - 108° = a° \rightarrow a° = 72°$

30) Choice B is correct

15% of 40: $\frac{15}{100} \times 40 = \frac{15\times40}{100} = \frac{600}{100} = 6$

31) Choice C is correct

$N = 2$ and $\frac{64}{N} + 4 = \square$

Then: $\frac{64}{2} + 4 = 32 + 4 = 36$

32) Choice D is correct

There are 30 days in 1 month. If $450 is the total amount paid in a month, the average amount paid per day is $450 \div 30 = \$15$

33) Choice A is correct

$-7a = 63 \rightarrow a = \frac{63}{-7} = -9$

34) Choice A is correct

$N \times (5 - 3) = 12 \rightarrow N(2) = 12 \rightarrow N = 6$

35) Choice B is correct

Review the choices provided.

A. $(x + y)z = xz + yz$

B. $x \div y = \left(\dfrac{x}{y}\right) = x\left(\dfrac{1}{y}\right) \neq y\left(\dfrac{1}{x}\right)$

C. $(x + y) \div z = \dfrac{x}{z} + \dfrac{y}{z}$

D. $x(y + 1) = xy + x$

36) Choice D is correct

$ON = 4 - (-6) = 10$ units. Let $x = OM$. Then $MN = 10 - x$. Substitute these expressions in the given equation: $x = \dfrac{1}{3}(10 - x)$. Solve for x:

$$x = \frac{10}{3} - \frac{x}{3} \rightarrow x + \frac{x}{3} = \frac{10}{3} \rightarrow \frac{4x}{3} = \frac{10}{3} \rightarrow 12x = 30 \rightarrow x = \frac{30}{12} = 2.5$$

37) Choice B is correct

$80(\$1.50) + 200(\$2.00) = \$520$

38) Choice A is correct

First, subtract $24 from $62: $62 - 26 = 36$

Then, divide by 3: $36 \div 3 = 12$

39) Choice B is correct

The point represents the $x -$ value of -3 and the $y -$ value of 3, thus the ordered pair may be written as $(-3, 3)$

40) Choice C is correct

$\dfrac{25}{10} = 2.5$

41) Choice D is correct

The first part of the problem may be modeled with the equation, $30 = 0.60x$, solving for x, gives $x = 50$. 20% of 50 may be written as 0.20×50, which equals 10.

42) Choice B is correct

Begin by adding 6 to 30. This number divided by 6 will provide the answer: $30 + 6 = 36 \rightarrow 36 \div 6 = 6$

43) Choice C is correct

This is done by ratios. The relationship between part of the room and the whole room is the same as the relationship between the time it takes to paint part of the room and the time it takes to paint the whole room $\rightarrow \frac{5}{x}$

44) Choice D is correct

Use FOIL method. $(2x + y)(x - 2y) = 2x^2 - 4xy + xy - 2y^2 = 2x^2 - 3xy - 2y^2$

45) Choice D is correct

Five to the fifth power $= 5^5$, $5^5 = 5 \times 5 \times 5 \times 5 \times 5 = 3{,}125$

46) Choice D is correct

To determine the ratio of the two fractions, multiply them by 10. $\frac{2}{5}$ to $\frac{3}{10} = 4$ to 3

47) Choice B is correct

Rename the fraction with a common denominator. Do the operations in parentheses first.

$$\left(\frac{5}{4} + \frac{2}{3}\right) - \left(\frac{1}{2} - \frac{1}{3}\right) = x \rightarrow \left(\frac{15}{12} + \frac{8}{12}\right) - \left(\frac{3}{6} - \frac{2}{6}\right) = x \rightarrow \frac{23}{12} - \frac{1}{6} = x \rightarrow \frac{23}{12} - \frac{2}{12} = \frac{21}{12} = \frac{7}{4}$$
$$= 1\frac{13}{4}$$

48) Choice B is correct

$(x + 2)(x + 3) = x^2 + 3x + 2x + 6 = x^2 + 5x + 6$

49) Choice B is correct

$(X) = 25$

$(Y) = 24$

$(Z) = 25$

So $(X) = (Z)$ and both are greater than (Y).

50) Choice C is correct

$(x^6)^4 = x^{6\times4} = x^{24}$

51) Choice B is correct

$\frac{(8\ feet\ +8\ yards)}{4} = \frac{(8\ feet\ +24\ feet\ )}{4} = \frac{(32\ feet\ )}{4} = 8$ feet

52) Choice C is correct

Convert everything an equation: $35 = 3 \times$ shirt -10

Now, solve the equation: $45 = 3$ shirt $\rightarrow$ shirt $= \frac{45}{3} = 15$

The shirt was $15.

53) Choice A is correct

Multiply and simplify. $\frac{4\times9}{5\times12} = \frac{36}{60} = \frac{3}{5}$

54) Choice C is correct

The millions begin with the seventh digit to the left of the decimal place. Because we need 435 million, we can immediately eliminate choices B and D. Road on: 800 thousand. We need look no further for the correct answer.

55) Choice B is correct

$6^2 = 36$. Because a is greater than 6, a^2 must be greater than 36. Obviously, then, a^2 is greater than 34.

56) Choice B is correct

Divide $\frac{5}{8}$ by $\frac{1}{4}$ to find the answer. $\frac{5}{8} \div \frac{1}{4} = \frac{5}{8} \times \frac{4}{1} = \frac{5}{2} = 2\frac{1}{2}$

57) Choice B is correct

Check each choices:

A. $(8 \times 10^3) + (6 \times 10^2) + 7 = 8,000 + 600 + 7 = 8,607$

B. $(8 \times 10^2) + (6 \times 10) + 7 = 8 + 60 + 3 = 867$

C. $(8 \times 10^3) + (6 \times 10^2) + (7 \times 10) = 8,000 + 600 + 70 = 8,670$

D. $(8 \times 10^3) + (6 \times 10) + 7 = 8,000 + 60 + 7 = 8,067$

Only choice B equal to 867.

58) Choice D is correct

For each doctor, there are 3 nurses. Let x be the number of nurses and set a proportion: $\frac{1}{3} = \frac{24}{x} \rightarrow x = 72$

59) Choice A is correct

Substitute the values into the expression.

$$\sqrt{3y + 2z + x} = \sqrt{3(3) + 2(5) + 6} = \sqrt{9 + 10 + 6} = \sqrt{25} = 5$$

60) Choice A is correct

6 is one-eighth of 48, and $\frac{3}{8}$ is one-eighth of 3.

61) Choice D is correct

$\sqrt[3]{216} = \sqrt[3]{6^3} = 6$

62) Choice B is correct

Plug in the value of x in the expression. Then: $6x^2 + 5x - 13 = 6(7)^2 + 5(7) - 13 = 316$

63) Choice C is correct

$(6 \times 10^2) + (2 \times 10) = 600 + 20 = 620$

$(7 \times 10^3) + 9 = 7,000 + 9 = 7,009$

The difference is: $7,009 - 620 = 6,389$

64) Choice B is correct

The formula of a triangle is $A = \frac{1}{2}bh = \frac{1}{2} \times 10 \; cm \times 16 \; cm = 80 \; cm^2$

HSPT Mathematics Practice Test 4

1) Choice D is correct

In order to solve for x, both sides of the equation may multiply by 7.

$$7\left(\frac{5x}{7}\right) = 7(10 - 5x) \rightarrow 5x = 70 - 35x \rightarrow 5x + 35x = 70 \rightarrow 40x = 70 \rightarrow x = \frac{70}{40} = \frac{7}{4}$$

2) Choice D is correct

A. $f(x) = x^2 - 5$ if $x = 1 \rightarrow f(1) = (1)^2 - 5 = 1 - 5 = -4 \neq 5$

B. $f(x) = x^2 - 1$ if $x = 1 \rightarrow f(1) = (1)^2 - 1 = 1 - 1 = 0 \neq 5$

C. $f(x) = \sqrt{x + 2}$ if $x = 1 \rightarrow f(1) = \sqrt{1 + 2} = \sqrt{3} \neq 5$

D. $f(x) = \sqrt{x} + 4$ if $x = 1 \rightarrow f(1) = \sqrt{1} + 4 = 5$

3) Choice B is correct

The value of x may be determined by dividing both side of the equation $a = 4x$ by 4. Doing so gives $\frac{a}{4} = x$. Substituting $\frac{a}{4}$ for the variable, x, in the equation $8x = 2b$, gives $8\left(\frac{a}{4}\right) = 2b \rightarrow$ $2a = 2b \rightarrow a = b$

4) Choice A is correct

When dividing terms with the same base, the exponents should be subtracted. Thus, $\frac{a^4}{a^2} = a^2$

5) Choice A is correct

Use PEMDAS (order of operation):

$$-18 + 6 \times (-5) - [4 + 22 \times (-4)] \div 2 = -18 - 30 - [4 - 88] \div 2 = -48 - [-84] \div 2$$
$$= -48 + 84 \div 2 = -48 + 42 = -6$$

6) Choice B is correct

Moving the decimal to the right of the digit, 2, gives the equivalent expression, 2.5×10^5, since there are 5 digits to the right of the 2.

7) Choice D is correct

The formula, $I = Prt$, represents the amount of interest earned, for a particular principal, interest rate, and amount of time. Substituting 200 for I, 5,000 for P and 0.06 for r gives:

$$200 = 4,000 \times 0.05 \times t \rightarrow 200 = 200t \rightarrow t = 1$$

8) Choice C is correct

Since angles x and y are complementary, the measure of angle y is equal to the difference of $90°$ and $32°$: $90 - 32 = 58 \rightarrow y = 58°$

9) Choice D is correct

Write factors of 45: $1, 3, 5, 9, 15, 45$. So, 12 is not a factor of 45.

10) Choice A is correct

When subtracting fractional numbers, you must first rename the numbers with a common denominator: $10 - 3\frac{4}{9} = \frac{90}{9} - \frac{31}{9} = \frac{59}{9} = 6\frac{5}{9}$

11) Choice A is correct

This can be set up an equation. If x equals the price of the laptop, 4% of x equals $50, or $0.04x = 50 \rightarrow x = \frac{50}{0.04} = 1,250$

12) Choice A is correct

Let x be the unknown integer. Then: $x + 12 = \frac{8}{7}x \rightarrow x - \frac{8}{7}x = -12 \rightarrow -\frac{1}{7}x = -12 \rightarrow x = 12 \times 7 = 84$

13) Choice D is correct

Because Mark is now 20, two years ago he was 18. His father was then 3 times older, or 54. Now, two years later, Mark's father is 56.

14) Choice A is correct

Replace the letters in the problem with the given numbers: $\frac{2yz}{3x} = \frac{2(6)(5)}{3(4)} = \frac{60}{12} = 5$

15) Choice C is correct

The cube of 6 divided by 6 is the square of 6. $\frac{6^3}{6} = 6^2 = 36 \rightarrow 36 - 5 = 31$

16) Choice C is correct

The differences of two numbers in the series so far are: $5, 6, 7$. Then, the next two numbers should be: $42 + 8 = 50, 50 + 9 = 59$

17) Choice A is correct

Use average formula: $\frac{24+19+65+88}{4} = 49 \rightarrow 49 - 38 = 11$

18) Choice D is correct

Let x be the number. $40\% + 20\% = 60\% = 0.60$

$0.60x = 84 \rightarrow x = 140$

19) Choice C is correct

Count the 2s and 3s carefully.

$2^5 = 2 \times 2 \times 2 \times 2 \times 2$

$6^3 = 6 \times 6 \times 6$

$2^5 \times 6^3 = 2 \times 2 \times 2 \times 2 \times 2 \times 6 \times 6 \times 6 = 2 \times 2 \times 2 \times 2 \times 6 \times 6 \times 18$

20) Choice B is correct

$(2x + 4)^{\circ}$ and 96° are vertical angles. Vertical angles are equal in measure.

$2x + 4 = 96 \rightarrow 2x = 92 \rightarrow x = 46^{\circ}$

21) Choice A is correct

Compare the digits in the hundredths place: $0 < 3$

22) Choice A is correct

$x^2 + 14 = 50 \rightarrow x^2 - 14 = 50 - 14 \rightarrow x^2 = 36 \rightarrow x = \pm 6$

23) Choice B is correct

The total number of degrees in a circle is 360. $30°$ of $360°$ is $\frac{30}{360}$ which reduces to $\frac{1}{12}$.

24) Choice A is correct

Area of square equals $(one\ side)^2 \rightarrow x^2 = 144\ cm^2 \rightarrow x = 12\ cm$

25) Choice B is correct

First calculate square of -3: $|-5| + 9 \times 2\frac{1}{3} + 9$

Convert mix number to fraction, then multiply to 9: $|-5| + \frac{63}{3} + 9$

Calculate absolute value and add terms: $5 + 21 + 9 = 35$

26) Choice D is correct

The three angles in a triangle always add up to $180°$. So, only choice D is correct.

$$40 + 50 + 90 = 180$$

27) Choice A is correct

First convert fractions to get decimals, then sort the decimals, greatest to lest:

$\frac{3}{4} = 0.75$, $\frac{2}{3} = 0.\bar{6}$, $\frac{4}{7} \approx 0.57$, $\frac{1}{2} = 0.5$, $\frac{2}{5} = 0.4 \rightarrow 0.75 > 0.\bar{6} > 0.57 > 0.5 > 0.4$

28) Choice B is correct

$-12 + (5 \times n) = 5n - 12$

29) Choice C is correct

Only choice C provides a correct answer. Substitute 2.5 for x:

A. $3(2.5) > 9.5 \rightarrow 7.5 > 9.5$

B. $4(2.5) = 9.78 \rightarrow 10 = 9.78$

C. $2(2.5) < 6 \rightarrow 5 < 6$

D. $5(2.5) - 1 > 12 \rightarrow 11 > 12$

30) Choice B is correct

1 liter equals to 1,000 ml, make a proportion: $\frac{1\,l}{x} = \frac{1,000\,ml}{650\,ml} \rightarrow 1,000x = 650 \rightarrow x = \frac{650}{1,000} = 0.65$

31) Choice A is correct

Let x be the number of girls in the class. Write a proportion and solve for x:

$\frac{3}{2} = \frac{27}{x} \rightarrow 3x = 54 \rightarrow x = 18$

32) Choice B is correct

$\left| -\frac{3}{2} \right| = \frac{3}{2} = 1.5$

Point B represents the value of $\left| -\frac{3}{2} \right|$.

33) Choice C is correct

The range of a set of data is the difference between the highest and lowest values in the set.
Then, the range of the set of data is: $36 - 3 = 33$

34) Choice D is correct

Multiply the numerators and denominators. Then simplify: $\frac{5}{18} \times \frac{9}{60} = \frac{45}{1080} = \frac{1}{24}$

35) Choice B is correct

A. $2(4) + 5 = 13$

B. $14 - 36 - 12 = -34$

C. $12 + 104 - 5 = 111$

D. $28 - 56 + 10 = -18$

Only choice B equals -34.

36) Choice C is correct

Let x to be height of triangle, then use this formula: $A = \frac{b \times h}{2} \rightarrow 36 = \frac{4 \times x}{2} \rightarrow 4x = 72 \rightarrow x = 18$.

37) Choice D is correct

$\frac{5}{8} = 0.625 = 62.50\%$

38) Choice C is correct

$1\ m = 100\ cm \rightarrow 2\ m = 200\ cm \rightarrow$ The height of tree in centimeters equals $240\ cm$

Convert centimeters to millimeters: $1\ cm = 10\ mm \rightarrow 240\ cm = 2{,}400\ mm$

39) Choice B is correct

A. $2(x + 3) = 2x + 6 \neq 2x + 5$

B. $2x - 5 + 8 + 5x = 7x + 3$

C. $10 \neq 20$

D. $26 \neq 20$

Only $2x - 5 + 8 + 5x$ and $7x + 3$ are equivalent

40) Choice B is correct

$\sqrt{64} = 8$

41) Choice A is correct

Total fluid of milk equals 13 ounces, he drank p fluid ounces of milk on Saturday morning, so the number of fluid ounces of milk he drank the rest of the weekend: $13 - p = q$.

42) Choice D is correct

Radius of a circle equals $\frac{diameter}{2} = \frac{18}{2} = 9\ cm$. Then the area of the circle:

$\pi r^2 = \pi(9^2) = 81 \times \pi\ cm$

43) Choice C is correct

$a^a . a = 4^4 . 4 = 256 . 4 = 1,024$

44) Choice C is correct

Marc's equation: $2\frac{2}{3} = \frac{8}{3} = \frac{24}{9} \neq \frac{16}{9}$, Tom's equation: $1.05 = \frac{105}{100} \neq \frac{105}{10}$

45) Choice B is correct

$7 + 2x \leq 15 \rightarrow 2x \leq 15 - 7 \rightarrow 2x \leq 8 \rightarrow x \leq 4$

46) Choice C is correct

Kevin finished the race in $9\ hr.\ 30\ min + 2\ hr.\ 15\ min = 11\ hr.\ 45\ min\ A.M.$

Nicole finished the race in $11\ hr.\ 45\ min + 1\ hr.\ 40\ min = 12\ hr.\ 85\ min,$

There are 60 minutes in an hour. Then: $12\ hr.\ 85\ min = 13\ hr.\ 25\ min = 1\ hr.\ 25\ min\ P.M.$

Nicole finished the race at: $1:25\ P.M.$

47) Choice B is correct

3.5 points for every correct answer, so the total number of points that he earned for answering q questions correctly $= 3.5q$. Only choice B provides the right equation.

48) Choice C is correct

In the fractions $\frac{2}{6} + \frac{3}{4}$, the first one represents a shape that is divided to 4 parts and 3 parts of it are shaded $(\frac{3}{4})$. The second fraction can be a picture that is divided into 6 parts that 2 parts of that is shaded $(\frac{2}{6})$. Only choice C provides those shapes.

49) Choice B is correct

Let's order number of pens in the boxes: $8, 13, 14, 20, 28, 32, 32, 36, 42, 45$

Median is the number in the middle. Since there are 10 numbers (an even number) the Median is the average of numbers 5 and 6: Median is: $\frac{28+32}{2} = 30.$

50) Choice C is correct

Consecutive numbers are numbers that follow in sequence. The answer with two consecutive numbers is choice C, because 8 comes after 7 on the number line.

51) Choice B is correct

The fraction that comes between $\frac{1}{4}$ and $\frac{3}{4}$, is $\frac{2}{4}$, which reduces to $\frac{1}{2}$.

52) Choice C is correct

Because ABC and AGH are similar, their corresponding sides are in the same proportions. The correct answer compares corresponding sides of each triangle.

$$\frac{AB}{AG} = \frac{BC}{GH}$$

53) Choice B is correct

The equation for the word problem is $x = (5 \times 2.40) + (3 \times 3.50) = 12 + 10.50 = 22.50$

54) Choice B is correct

The associative property of addition states that you can add the same numbers in different orders and still get the same sum. Choice B demonstrates that this property is true.

55) Choice B is correct

Square both sides of the equation and solve for x:

$$\sqrt{x - 15} = 7 \rightarrow x - 15 = 49 \rightarrow x = 49 + 15 \rightarrow x = 64$$

56) Choice D is correct

Eliminate choices A and C because they're even numbers. x is less than 9, which means it can't equal to 9. So, choice D is correct.

57) Choice A is correct

$12 + 113 = x^3 \rightarrow 125 = x^3$. The cube root of 125 is 5.

58) Choice C is correct

The value of the angle next to the $138°$: $180° - 138° = 42°$

www.EffortlessMath.com

The angles inside a triangle also add up to $180°$: $32 + 42 + x = 180 \rightarrow x = 106$

59) Choice C is correct

$\frac{13}{5}$ as a mixed number is $2\frac{3}{5}$. The integers between $2\frac{3}{5}$ and 6.4 are $3, 4, 5$ and 6, which makes choice C the answer.

60) Choice D is correct

The only perfect square among the choices is 169, choice D; its 13^2.

61) Choice D is correct

$a - b = 6 \rightarrow a - b > 0$

62) Choice D is correct

Recall the formula for the volume of a cube: s^3 is 5^3, or $125 \ in^3$.

63) Choice B is correct

There are 6 triangles and 2 of them are shaded. The fraction of the shaded area is $\frac{2}{6}$, which simplifies to $\frac{1}{3}$.

64) Choice B is correct

Create an equation and solve for x. Because the ratios of the two numbers is 3 to 2, we can express the two numbers as $3x$ and $2x$.

$3x + 2x = 45 \rightarrow 5x = 45 \rightarrow x = 9$

The smaller number is $2x = 2(9) = 18$

HSPT Mathematics Practice Test 5

1)   Choice A is correct

Convert the mixed numbers into improper fractions. Then divide:

$$\frac{4\frac{3}{9}}{2\frac{1}{6}} = \frac{\frac{39}{9}}{\frac{13}{6}} = \frac{39}{9} \div \frac{13}{6} = \frac{39}{9} \times \frac{6}{13} = 2$$

2)   Choice D is correct

First determine how many times $18,000 can be divided by 100: $18,000 \div 100 = 180$

For every $100 in $18,000, $2.15 must be paid in taxes: $180 \times 2.15 = \$387$

3)   Choice C is correct

40% of 70 equals: $0.40 \times 70 = 28$. And 10 less than that is: $28 - 10 = 18$

4)   Choice D is correct

A centimeter consists of 10 millimeters, and a meter consist of 100 centimeters:

$1 \times 10 \times 100 = 1,000$.

5)   Choice B is correct

Let x be the regular price. $0.15x = 6 \rightarrow x = \frac{6}{0.15} = 40$

6)   Choice B is correct

Add 53 to both sides of the equation: $5x - 53 + 53 = 22 + 53 \rightarrow 5x = 75$

Divide both sides of equation by 5: $x = 15$

7)   Choice B is correct

The diameter of the smaller circle $= 17 - 2 - 7 = 8\ mm$,

Then: the radius of the smaller circle $= 8 \div 2 = 4\ mm$.

8)   Choice C is correct

Use the PEMDAS order of operation:

www.EffortlessMath.com

Calculate within parentheses $(8 + 4^2) = 24$ and $(18 \div 3) = 6$

Then: $24 \div 6 = 4$

9) Choice B is correct

Write the numbers in order: $5, 6, 9, 10, 14, 16, 19$

Since we have 7 numbers (7 is odd), then the median is the number in the middle, which is 10.

10) Choice D is correct

Wood and glass make up 85% of a sculpture. Then: $w + g = 85$

The percentage of the sculpture that is made of wood: $w = 85 - g$

11) Choice C is correct

The ratio of lions to tigers is 12 to 4 or 3 to 1 at the zoo. Therefore, total number of lions and tigers must be divisible by 4. $3 + 1 = 4$, From the numbers provided, only 98 is not divisible by 4.

12) Choice D is correct

$15 - 25 = -10$, The temperature at midnight was 10 degrees below zero.

13) Choice D is correct

Distance $= speed \times time \Rightarrow time = \frac{distance}{speed} = \frac{480}{40} = 12$. The trip takes 12 hours. Change hours to minutes, then: $12 \times 60 = 720$

14) Choice B is correct

$8(a - 3) = 16$, Divide both sides by 8: $\frac{8(a-3)}{8} = \frac{16}{8} \rightarrow a - 3 = 2$

Add 3 to both sides: $a - 3 + 3 = 2 + 3 \rightarrow a = 5$

15) Choice D is correct

There are equal numbers of four types of cards. Therefore, the total number of cards must be divisible by 4. Only choice D (56) is divisible by 4.

16) Choice D is correct

Use exponent multiplication rule: $x^a \times x^b = x^{a+b}$

Then: $3^{24} = 3^8 \times 3^x = 3^{8+x}$

$24 = 8 + x \Rightarrow x = 24 - 8 = 16$

17) Choice C is correct

$\frac{1.75}{1.40} = 1.25 = 125\%$

18) Choice D is correct

$\sqrt[8]{256} = 2$, $(2^8 = 2 \times 2 \times 2 \times 2 \times 2 \times 2 \times 2 \times 2 = 256)$

19) Choice C is correct

$\sqrt{81} = 9$, $\sqrt{64} = 8$, Then: $9 \times 8 = 72$

20) Choice A is correct

Since Julie gives 6 pieces of candy to each of her friends, then, then number of pieces of candies must be divisible by 6.

A. $180 \div 6 = 30$

B. $217 \div 6 = 36.16$

C. $243 \div 6 = 40.5$

D. $263 \div 6 = 43.83$

Only choice A gives a whole number.

21) Choice A is correct

Diameter $= 18$, then: Radius $= 9$

Area of a circle $= \pi r^2 \Rightarrow A = 3.14(9)^2 = 245.34$

22) Choice C is correct

If $a = 4$ then: $b = \frac{a^2}{4} + 2 \Rightarrow b = \frac{4^2}{4} + 2 = 4 + 2 = 6$

23) Choice A is correct

An obtuse angle is an angle of greater than 90 degrees and less than 180 degrees. Only choice A is an obtuse angle.

24) Choice C is correct

From the list of numbers, 11, 13, and 19 are prime numbers. Their sum is:

$11 + 13 + 19 = 43$

25) Choice D is correct

105 divided by 6, the remainder is 3. 87 divided by 4, the remainder is also 3.

26) Choice D is correct

Area $= side^2 \rightarrow 81 = side^2 \rightarrow side = 9$

Perimeter $= 4side \rightarrow Perimeter = 4 \times 9 = 36$

27) Choice B is correct

Factor the number: $3,375 = 15^3$, $\sqrt[3]{15^3} = 15$, Then: $\sqrt[3]{3,375} = 15$

28) Choice D is correct

To solve this problem, divide $5\frac{1}{2}$ by $\frac{1}{6}$. $5\frac{1}{2} \div \frac{1}{6} = \frac{11}{2} \div \frac{1}{6} = \frac{11}{2} \times \frac{6}{1} = 33$

29) Choice B is correct

Slope of a line: $\frac{y_2 - y_1}{x_2 - x_1} = \frac{rise}{run} \rightarrow \frac{y_2 - y_1}{x_2 - x_1} = \frac{3 - 7}{5 - 6} = \frac{-4}{-1} = 4$

30) Choice D is correct

$3.26 + 15.69 + 2.50 + 4.66 + 17.99 = 44.1$

31) Choice C is correct

The digit 6 has a value of $6 \times \frac{1}{100}$, The digit 4 has a value of $4 \times 10,000$, The digit 8 has a value of $8 \times 10 = 800$, The digit 5 has a value of $9 \times 1,000$. Only choice C is correct.

32) Choice B is correct

Apply the exponent rule: $(a.b)^n = a^n.b^n \rightarrow 3(4x^5)^3 = 3 \times 4^3 \times (x^5)^3 =$

Apply the exponent rule: $(a^m)^n = a^{m \times n} \rightarrow (x^5)^3 = x^{15}$

then: $3 \times 4^3 \times (x^5)^3 = 3 \times 64 \times x^{15} = 192 \times x^{15} = 192x^{15}$

33) Choice D is correct

N is even. Let's choose 2 and 4 for N. Now, let's review the options provided.

A. $\frac{N}{2} = \frac{2}{2} = 1$, $\frac{N}{2} = \frac{4}{2} = 2$,   One result is odd and the other one is even.

B. $N + 4 = 2 + 4 = 6$, $4 + 4 = 8$ Both results are even.

C. $2N = 2 \times 2 = 4$, $4 \times 2 = 8$ Both results are even.

D. $N + 1 = 2 + 1 = 3$, $4 + 1 = 5$ Both results are odd.

34) Choice D is correct

Four people can paint 4 houses in 10 days. It means that for painting 8 houses in 10 days we need 8 people. To paint 8 houses in 5 days, 16 people are needed.

35) Choice D is correct

A quadrilateral with one pair of parallel sides is a trapezoid.

36) Choice B is correct

1 pizza has 8 slices. 19 pizzas contain (19×8) 152 slices

37) Choice A is correct

The length of MN is equal to: $2x + 6x = 8x$. Then: $8x = 32 \rightarrow x = \frac{32}{8} = 4$

ON is equal to: $6x = 6(4) = 24$

38) Choice C is correct

$\frac{1 \; hour}{18 \; coffees} = \frac{x}{1,800} \Rightarrow 18 \times x = 1 \times 1,800 \Rightarrow 18x = 1,800 \Rightarrow x = 100$

It takes 100 hours until she's made 1,800 coffees.

39) Choice D is correct

The two triangles are similar. So, set up a proportion to solve for x: $\frac{x+8}{x} = \frac{6}{4} \rightarrow 4(x+8) = 6x \rightarrow 32 = 2x \rightarrow x = 16$

40) Choice C is correct

Use simple interest formula: $I = prt \rightarrow I = (8,000)(0.045)(5) = 1,800$

41) Choice D is correct

Some of prime numbers are: $2, 3, 5, 7, 11, 13$

Find the product of two consecutive prime numbers:

$2 \times 3 = 6$ (not in the options)

$3 \times 5 = 15$ (bingo!)

$5 \times 7 = 35$ (not in the options)

$7 \times 11 = 77$ (not in the options)

42) Choice C is correct

Let's compare each fraction: $\frac{1}{7} < \frac{3}{8} < \frac{5}{11} < \frac{3}{4}$

Only choice C provides the right order.

43) Choice B is correct

Let x be the smallest number. Then, these are the numbers: $x, x+1, x+2, x+3, x+4$

Average $= \frac{sum\ of\ terms}{number\ of\ terms} \Rightarrow 38 = \frac{x+(x+1)+(x+2)+(x+3)+(x+4)}{5} \Rightarrow 38 = \frac{5x+10}{5} \Rightarrow 190 = 5x + 10$

$\Rightarrow 180 = 5x \Rightarrow x = 36$

44) Choice D is correct

In the figure angle A is labeled $(3x - 2)$ and it measures 37. Thus, $3x - 2 = 37$ and $3x = 39$ or $x = 13$.

That means that angle B, which is labeled $(5x)$, must measure $5 \times 13 = 65$.

Since the three angles of a triangle must add up to 180,

$37 + 65 + y - 8 = 180$, then: $y + 94 = 108 \rightarrow y = 180 - 94 = 86$

45) Choice D is correct

$4! \times 5 = 4 \times 3 \times 2 \times 1 \times 5 = 120$

46) Choice D is correct

8 chairs for every 4 desks, then: $\frac{8}{4} = 2 \rightarrow 2$ chairs for one desk

$50 \times 2 = 100 \rightarrow 100$ chairs for every 50 desks

47) Choice A is correct

The area of a 14 feet $\times$ 14 feet room is 196 square feet. $14 \times 14 = 196$

48) Choice A is correct

$2y + 4y + 2y = -24 \Rightarrow 8y = -24 \Rightarrow y = -\frac{24}{8} \Rightarrow y = -3$

49) Choice A is correct

$150 - 30 = 120 \rightarrow$ rooms painted, Then: $average = \frac{120}{8} = 15$

50) Choice B is correct

Subtract $\frac{1}{6b}$ and $\frac{1}{b^2}$ from both sides of the equation. Then:

$\frac{1}{6b^2} + \frac{1}{6b} = \frac{1}{b^2} \rightarrow \frac{1}{6b^2} - \frac{1}{b^2} = -\frac{1}{6b}$

Multiply both numerator and denominator of the fraction $\frac{1}{b^2}$ by 6. Then: $\frac{1}{6b^2} - \frac{6}{6b^2} = -\frac{1}{6b}$

Simplify the first side of the equation: $-\frac{5}{6b^2} = -\frac{1}{6b}$

Use cross multiplication method: $30b = 6b^2 \rightarrow 30 = 6b \rightarrow b = 5$

51) Choice C is correct

The square of a number is $\frac{36}{64}$, then the number is the square root of $\frac{36}{64}$

$\sqrt{\frac{36}{64}} = \frac{6}{8}$, The cube of the number is: $(\frac{6}{8})^3 = \frac{216}{512}$

52) Choice C is correct

Use distance formula: $d = \sqrt{(x_1 - x_2)^2 + (y_1 - y_2)^2} = \sqrt{(1 - (-2))^2 + (3 - 7)^2}$

$\sqrt{9 + 16} = \sqrt{25} = 5$

53) Choice D is correct

122 is not prime number, it is divided by 2

54) Choice C is correct

2 weeks $= 14$ days , 4 hours$\times 14$ days $= 56$ hours

56 hours $= 3,360$ minutes

55) Choice B is correct

$x^2 - 49 = 0 \Rightarrow x^2 = 49 \Rightarrow x$ could be 7 or -7.

56) Choice D is correct

Use Pythagorean Theorem: $a^2 + b^2 = c^2$

$(6)^2 + (8)^2 = c^2 \rightarrow 36 + 64 = 100 = c^2 \rightarrow C = \sqrt{100} = 10$

57) Choice A is correct

Average $= \frac{sum\ of\ terms}{number\ of\ terms} \Rightarrow 20 = \frac{14+16+21+x}{4} \Rightarrow 80 = 51 + x \Rightarrow x = 29$

58) Choice A is correct

$\frac{25}{50} = 0.5 = 50\%$

59) Choice A is correct

$x + 2y = 4$. Plug in the values of x and y from choices provided. Then:

A. $(-2, 3)$: $x + 2y = 4 \rightarrow -2 + 2(3) = 4 \rightarrow -2 + 6 = 4$ This is true!

B. $(1, 2)$: $x + 2y = 4 \rightarrow 1 + 2(2) = 4 \rightarrow 1 + 4 = 5$ This is NOT true!

C. $(-1, 3)$: $x + 2y = 4 \rightarrow -1 + 2(3) = 4 \rightarrow -1 + 6 = 5$ This is NOT true!

D. $(-3, 4)$: $x + 2y = 4 \rightarrow -3 + 2(4) = 4 \rightarrow -3 + 8 = 5$ This is NOT true!

60) Choice D is correct

$2x - 6 = 4.5 \rightarrow 2x = 4.5 + 6 \rightarrow 2x = 10.5 \rightarrow x = 5.25$

Then; $8x - 2 = 8(5.25) - 2 = 40$

61) Choice A is correct

$x = 25 + 135 = 160$

62) Choice A is correct

The width of the rectangle is twice its length. Let x be the length. Then, $width = 2x$

Perimeter of the rectangle is: $2\ (width\ +\ length) =$

$2(2x + x) = 66 \rightarrow 6x = 66 \rightarrow x = 11$, Length of the rectangle is 11 meters.

63) Choice D is correct

To get a sum of 6 for two dice, we can get 5 different options:

$$(5,1), (4,2), (3,3), (2,4), (1,5)$$

To get a sum of 9 for two dice, we can get 4 different options:

$$(6,3), (5,4), (4,5), (3,6)$$

Therefore, there are 9 options to get the sum of 6 or 9.

Since, we have $6 \times 6 = 36$ total options, the probability of getting a sum of 6 and 9 is 9 out of 36 or $\frac{1}{4}$.

64) Choice C is correct

$\sqrt{16x^2} = \sqrt{16} \times \sqrt{x^2} = 4 \times x = 4x$

"Effortless Math Education" Publications

Effortless Math authors' team strives to prepare and publish the best quality Mathematics learning resources to make learning Math easier for all. We hope that our publications help you learn Math in an effective way and prepare for the test.

We all in Effortless Math wish you good luck and successful studies!

Effortless Math Authors

www.EffortlessMath.com

... So Much More Online!

✓ FREE HSPT Math lessons

✓ More HSPT Math books!

✓ HSPT Mathematics Worksheets

✓ Online Math Tutors

Need a PDF version of this book?

Visit www.EffortlessMath.com

Receive the PDF version of this book or get another FREE book!

Thank you for using our Book!

Do you LOVE this book?

Then, you can get the PDF version of this book or another book absolutely FREE!

Please email us at:

info@EffortlessMath.com

for details.

Made in the USA
Las Vegas, NV
19 July 2022

51830827R00070